C-669 CAREER EXAMINATION SERIES

This is your
PASSBOOK for...

Recreation Leader

Test Preparation Study Guide
Questions & Answers

NATIONAL LEARNING CORPORATION®

COPYRIGHT NOTICE

This book is SOLELY intended for, is sold ONLY to, and its use is RESTRICTED to individual, bona fide applicants or candidates who qualify by virtue of having seriously filed applications for appropriate license, certificate, professional and/or promotional advancement, higher school matriculation, scholarship, or other legitimate requirements of education and/or governmental authorities.

This book is NOT intended for use, class instruction, tutoring, training, duplication, copying, reprinting, excerption, or adaptation, etc., by:

1) Other publishers
2) Proprietors and/or Instructors of "Coaching" and/or Preparatory Courses
3) Personnel and/or Training Divisions of commercial, industrial, and governmental organizations
4) Schools, colleges, or universities and/or their departments and staffs, including teachers and other personnel
5) Testing Agencies or Bureaus
6) Study groups which seek by the purchase of a single volume to copy and/or duplicate and/or adapt this material for use by the group as a whole without having purchased individual volumes for each of the members of the group
7) Et al.

Such persons would be in violation of appropriate Federal and State statutes.

PROVISION OF LICENSING AGREEMENTS – Recognized educational, commercial, industrial, and governmental institutions and organizations, and others legitimately engaged in educational pursuits, including training, testing, and measurement activities, may address request for a licensing agreement to the copyright owners, who will determine whether, and under what conditions, including fees and charges, the materials in this book may be used them. In other words, a licensing facility exists for the legitimate use of the material in this book on other than an individual basis. However, it is asseverated and affirmed here that the material in this book CANNOT be used without the receipt of the express permission of such a licensing agreement from the Publishers. Inquiries re licensing should be addressed to the company, attention rights and permissions department.

All rights reserved, including the right of reproduction in whole or in part, in any form or by any means, electronic or mechanical, including photocopying, recording, or by any information storage and retrieval system, without permission in writing from the Publisher.

Copyright © 2025 by
National Learning Corporation

212 Michael Drive, Syosset, NY 11791
(516) 921-8888 • www.passbooks.com
E-mail: info@passbooks.com

PASSBOOK® SERIES

THE *PASSBOOK® SERIES* has been created to prepare applicants and candidates for the ultimate academic battlefield – the examination room.

At some time in our lives, each and every one of us may be required to take an examination – for validation, matriculation, admission, qualification, registration, certification, or licensure.

Based on the assumption that every applicant or candidate has met the basic formal educational standards, has taken the required number of courses, and read the necessary texts, the *PASSBOOK® SERIES* furnishes the one special preparation which may assure passing with confidence, instead of failing with insecurity. Examination questions – together with answers – are furnished as the basic vehicle for study so that the mysteries of the examination and its compounding difficulties may be eliminated or diminished by a sure method.

This book is meant to help you pass your examination provided that you qualify and are serious in your objective.

The entire field is reviewed through the huge store of content information which is succinctly presented through a provocative and challenging approach – the question-and-answer method.

A climate of success is established by furnishing the correct answers at the end of each test.

You soon learn to recognize types of questions, forms of questions, and patterns of questioning. You may even begin to anticipate expected outcomes.

You perceive that many questions are repeated or adapted so that you can gain acute insights, which may enable you to score many sure points.

You learn how to confront new questions, or types of questions, and to attack them confidently and work out the correct answers.

You note objectives and emphases, and recognize pitfalls and dangers, so that you may make positive educational adjustments.

Moreover, you are kept fully informed in relation to new concepts, methods, practices, and directions in the field.

You discover that you are actually taking the examination all the time: you are preparing for the examination by "taking" an examination, not by reading extraneous and/or supererogatory textbooks.

In short, this PASSBOOK®, used directedly, should be an important factor in helping you to pass your test.

RECREATION LEADER

DUTIES:

Under the general supervision of a higher level recreation employee, an incumbent in this class has responsibility for the organization and personal direction of a variety of recreation activities in a particular phase of the recreation program, within the guidelines and specific policies of that program. The Recreation Leader conducts activities with assigned groups of all ages, in varying programs and in different indoor/outdoor facilities or centers. An employee in this class is responsible for conducting a variety of activities at a recreation facility. The incumbent is required to work with all age groups in a firm and tactful manner, and must also possess the ability to rapidly acquire knowledge of the rules and objectives of a variety of games, hobbies and sports. Work is performed in accordance with a predetermined recreation program. Work is reviewed for adherence to departmental standards and program objective through observation, written reports and conferences. This position is distinguished from that of Senior Recreation Leader by the degree of responsibility and level of independent judgment utilized. Supervision may be exercised over subordinate personnel, including seasonal and volunteer staff. Does related work as required.

SUBJECT OF EXAMINATION:

The written test designed to evaluate knowledge, skills and /or abilities in the following areas:

1. **Office record keeping** - These questions test your ability to perform common office record keeping tasks, The test consists of two or more "sets" of questions, each set concerning a different problem. Typical record keeping problems might involve the organization or collation of data from several sources; scheduling; maintaining a record system using running balances; or completion of a table summarizing data using totals, subtotals, averages and percents.

2. **Principles and practices of leisure recreation** - These questions test for a knowledge of the basic concepts and common practices employed in the planning and implementation of leisure-time recreation programs in athletics, social activities, and avocational interests, Questions may cover such areas as program/activity planning for the major user groups, program/activity planning for people with special needs; operation of recreation areas, recreation center buildings, and specialized recreation facilities (pools, tennis courts, etc.); and scheduling of activities.

3. **Working with people to facilitate recreation and/or leisure activities** - These questions will test for the knowledge and abilities necessary to work with individuals of all backgrounds in the context of providing recreation and leisure activities. Questions may cover such areas as: human behavior and development, handling difficult situations, engaging and motivating participants, building rapport with participants, working with volunteers, and planning appropriate activities for participant group.

HOW TO TAKE A TEST

I. YOU MUST PASS AN EXAMINATION

A. *WHAT EVERY CANDIDATE SHOULD KNOW*

Examination applicants often ask us for help in preparing for the written test. What can I study in advance? What kinds of questions will be asked? How will the test be given? How will the papers be graded?

As an applicant for a civil service examination, you may be wondering about some of these things. Our purpose here is to suggest effective methods of advance study and to describe civil service examinations.

Your chances for success on this examination can be increased if you know how to prepare. Those "pre-examination jitters" can be reduced if you know what to expect. You can even experience an adventure in good citizenship if you know why civil service exams are given.

B. *WHY ARE CIVIL SERVICE EXAMINATIONS GIVEN?*

Civil service examinations are important to you in two ways. As a citizen, you want public jobs filled by employees who know how to do their work. As a job seeker, you want a fair chance to compete for that job on an equal footing with other candidates. The best-known means of accomplishing this two-fold goal is the competitive examination.

Exams are widely publicized throughout the nation. They may be administered for jobs in federal, state, city, municipal, town or village governments or agencies.

Any citizen may apply, with some limitations, such as the age or residence of applicants. Your experience and education may be reviewed to see whether you meet the requirements for the particular examination. When these requirements exist, they are reasonable and applied consistently to all applicants. Thus, a competitive examination may cause you some uneasiness now, but it is your privilege and safeguard.

C. *HOW ARE CIVIL SERVICE EXAMS DEVELOPED?*

Examinations are carefully written by trained technicians who are specialists in the field known as "psychological measurement," in consultation with recognized authorities in the field of work that the test will cover. These experts recommend the subject matter areas or skills to be tested; only those knowledges or skills important to your success on the job are included. The most reliable books and source materials available are used as references. Together, the experts and technicians judge the difficulty level of the questions.

Test technicians know how to phrase questions so that the problem is clearly stated. Their ethics do not permit "trick" or "catch" questions. Questions may have been tried out on sample groups, or subjected to statistical analysis, to determine their usefulness.

Written tests are often used in combination with performance tests, ratings of training and experience, and oral interviews. All of these measures combine to form the best-known means of finding the right person for the right job.

II. HOW TO PASS THE WRITTEN TEST

A. NATURE OF THE EXAMINATION

To prepare intelligently for civil service examinations, you should know how they differ from school examinations you have taken. In school you were assigned certain definite pages to read or subjects to cover. The examination questions were quite detailed and usually emphasized memory. Civil service exams, on the other hand, try to discover your present ability to perform the duties of a position, plus your potentiality to learn these duties. In other words, a civil service exam attempts to predict how successful you will be. Questions cover such a broad area that they cannot be as minute and detailed as school exam questions.

In the public service similar kinds of work, or positions, are grouped together in one "class." This process is known as *position-classification*. All the positions in a class are paid according to the salary range for that class. One class title covers all of these positions, and they are all tested by the same examination.

B. FOUR BASIC STEPS

1) Study the announcement

How, then, can you know what subjects to study? Our best answer is: "Learn as much as possible about the class of positions for which you've applied." The exam will test the knowledge, skills and abilities needed to do the work.

Your most valuable source of information about the position you want is the official exam announcement. This announcement lists the training and experience qualifications. Check these standards and apply only if you come reasonably close to meeting them.

The brief description of the position in the examination announcement offers some clues to the subjects which will be tested. Think about the job itself. Review the duties in your mind. Can you perform them, or are there some in which you are rusty? Fill in the blank spots in your preparation.

Many jurisdictions preview the written test in the exam announcement by including a section called "Knowledge and Abilities Required," "Scope of the Examination," or some similar heading. Here you will find out specifically what fields will be tested.

2) Review your own background

Once you learn in general what the position is all about, and what you need to know to do the work, ask yourself which subjects you already know fairly well and which need improvement. You may wonder whether to concentrate on improving your strong areas or on building some background in your fields of weakness. When the announcement has specified "some knowledge" or "considerable knowledge," or has used adjectives like "beginning principles of…" or "advanced … methods," you can get a clue as to the number and difficulty of questions to be asked in any given field. More questions, and hence broader coverage, would be included for those subjects which are more important in the work. Now weigh your strengths and weaknesses against the job requirements and prepare accordingly.

3) Determine the level of the position

Another way to tell how intensively you should prepare is to understand the level of the job for which you are applying. Is it the entering level? In other words, is this the position in which beginners in a field of work are hired? Or is it an intermediate or advanced level? Sometimes this is indicated by such words as "Junior" or "Senior" in the class title. Other jurisdictions use Roman numerals to designate the level – Clerk I, Clerk II, for example. The word "Supervisor" sometimes appears in the title. If the level is not indicated by the title, check the description of duties. Will you be working under very close supervision, or will you have responsibility for independent decisions in this work?

4) Choose appropriate study materials

Now that you know the subjects to be examined and the relative amount of each subject to be covered, you can choose suitable study materials. For beginning level jobs, or even advanced ones, if you have a pronounced weakness in some aspect of your training, read a modern, standard textbook in that field. Be sure it is up to date and has general coverage. Such books are normally available at your library, and the librarian will be glad to help you locate one. For entry-level positions, questions of appropriate difficulty are chosen – neither highly advanced questions, nor those too simple. Such questions require careful thought but not advanced training.

If the position for which you are applying is technical or advanced, you will read more advanced, specialized material. If you are already familiar with the basic principles of your field, elementary textbooks would waste your time. Concentrate on advanced textbooks and technical periodicals. Think through the concepts and review difficult problems in your field.

These are all general sources. You can get more ideas on your own initiative, following these leads. For example, training manuals and publications of the government agency which employs workers in your field can be useful, particularly for technical and professional positions. A letter or visit to the government department involved may result in more specific study suggestions, and certainly will provide you with a more definite idea of the exact nature of the position you are seeking.

III. KINDS OF TESTS

Tests are used for purposes other than measuring knowledge and ability to perform specified duties. For some positions, it is equally important to test ability to make adjustments to new situations or to profit from training. In others, basic mental abilities not dependent on information are essential. Questions which test these things may not appear as pertinent to the duties of the position as those which test for knowledge and information. Yet they are often highly important parts of a fair examination. For very general questions, it is almost impossible to help you direct your study efforts. What we can do is to point out some of the more common of these general abilities needed in public service positions and describe some typical questions.

1) General information

Broad, general information has been found useful for predicting job success in some kinds of work. This is tested in a variety of ways, from vocabulary lists to questions about current events. Basic background in some field of work, such as sociology or economics, may be sampled in a group of questions. Often these are principles which have become familiar to most persons through exposure rather than through formal training. It is difficult to advise you how to study for these questions; being alert to the world around you is our best suggestion.

2) Verbal ability

An example of an ability needed in many positions is verbal or language ability. Verbal ability is, in brief, the ability to use and understand words. Vocabulary and grammar tests are typical measures of this ability. Reading comprehension or paragraph interpretation questions are common in many kinds of civil service tests. You are given a paragraph of written material and asked to find its central meaning.

3) Numerical ability

Number skills can be tested by the familiar arithmetic problem, by checking paired lists of numbers to see which are alike and which are different, or by interpreting charts and graphs. In the latter test, a graph may be printed in the test booklet which you are asked to use as the basis for answering questions.

4) Observation

A popular test for law-enforcement positions is the observation test. A picture is shown to you for several minutes, then taken away. Questions about the picture test your ability to observe both details and larger elements.

5) Following directions

In many positions in the public service, the employee must be able to carry out written instructions dependably and accurately. You may be given a chart with several columns, each column listing a variety of information. The questions require you to carry out directions involving the information given in the chart.

6) Skills and aptitudes

Performance tests effectively measure some manual skills and aptitudes. When the skill is one in which you are trained, such as typing or shorthand, you can practice. These tests are often very much like those given in business school or high school courses. For many of the other skills and aptitudes, however, no short-time preparation can be made. Skills and abilities natural to you or that you have developed throughout your lifetime are being tested.

Many of the general questions just described provide all the data needed to answer the questions and ask you to use your reasoning ability to find the answers. Your best preparation for these tests, as well as for tests of facts and ideas, is to be at your physical and mental best. You, no doubt, have your own methods of getting into an exam-taking mood and keeping "in shape." The next section lists some ideas on this subject.

IV. KINDS OF QUESTIONS

Only rarely is the "essay" question, which you answer in narrative form, used in civil service tests. Civil service tests are usually of the short-answer type. Full instructions for answering these questions will be given to you at the examination. But in case this is your first experience with short-answer questions and separate answer sheets, here is what you need to know:

1) Multiple-choice Questions

Most popular of the short-answer questions is the "multiple choice" or "best answer" question. It can be used, for example, to test for factual knowledge, ability to solve problems or judgment in meeting situations found at work.

A multiple-choice question is normally one of three types—
- It can begin with an incomplete statement followed by several possible endings. You are to find the one ending which *best* completes the statement, although some of the others may not be entirely wrong.
- It can also be a complete statement in the form of a question which is answered by choosing one of the statements listed.

- It can be in the form of a problem – again you select the best answer.

Here is an example of a multiple-choice question with a discussion which should give you some clues as to the method for choosing the right answer:

When an employee has a complaint about his assignment, the action which will *best* help him overcome his difficulty is to
- A. discuss his difficulty with his coworkers
- B. take the problem to the head of the organization
- C. take the problem to the person who gave him the assignment
- D. say nothing to anyone about his complaint

In answering this question, you should study each of the choices to find which is best. Consider choice "A" – Certainly an employee may discuss his complaint with fellow employees, but no change or improvement can result, and the complaint remains unresolved. Choice "B" is a poor choice since the head of the organization probably does not know what assignment you have been given, and taking your problem to him is known as "going over the head" of the supervisor. The supervisor, or person who made the assignment, is the person who can clarify it or correct any injustice. Choice "C" is, therefore, correct. To say nothing, as in choice "D," is unwise. Supervisors have and interest in knowing the problems employees are facing, and the employee is seeking a solution to his problem.

2) True/False Questions

The "true/false" or "right/wrong" form of question is sometimes used. Here a complete statement is given. Your job is to decide whether the statement is right or wrong.

SAMPLE: A roaming cell-phone call to a nearby city costs less than a non-roaming call to a distant city.

This statement is wrong, or false, since roaming calls are more expensive.

This is not a complete list of all possible question forms, although most of the others are variations of these common types. You will always get complete directions for answering questions. Be sure you understand *how* to mark your answers – ask questions until you do.

V. RECORDING YOUR ANSWERS

Computer terminals are used more and more today for many different kinds of exams.

For an examination with very few applicants, you may be told to record your answers in the test booklet itself. Separate answer sheets are much more common. If this separate answer sheet is to be scored by machine – and this is often the case – it is highly important that you mark your answers correctly in order to get credit.

An electronic scoring machine is often used in civil service offices because of the speed with which papers can be scored. Machine-scored answer sheets must be marked with a pencil, which will be given to you. This pencil has a high graphite content which responds to the electronic scoring machine. As a matter of fact, stray dots may register as answers, so do not let your pencil rest on the answer sheet while you are pondering the correct answer. Also, if your pencil lead breaks or is otherwise defective, ask for another.

Since the answer sheet will be dropped in a slot in the scoring machine, be careful not to bend the corners or get the paper crumpled.

The answer sheet normally has five vertical columns of numbers, with 30 numbers to a column. These numbers correspond to the question numbers in your test booklet. After each number, going across the page are four or five pairs of dotted lines. These short dotted lines have small letters or numbers above them. The first two pairs may also have a "T" or "F" above the letters. This indicates that the first two pairs only are to be used if the questions are of the true-false type. If the questions are multiple choice, disregard the "T" and "F" and pay attention only to the small letters or numbers.

Answer your questions in the manner of the sample that follows:

32. The largest city in the United States is
    A. Washington, D.C.
    B. New York City
    C. Chicago
    D. Detroit
    E. San Francisco

1) Choose the answer you think is best. (New York City is the largest, so "B" is correct.)
2) Find the row of dotted lines numbered the same as the question you are answering. (Find row number 32)
3) Find the pair of dotted lines corresponding to the answer. (Find the pair of lines under the mark "B.")
4) Make a solid black mark between the dotted lines.

VI. BEFORE THE TEST

Common sense will help you find procedures to follow to get ready for an examination. Too many of us, however, overlook these sensible measures. Indeed, nervousness and fatigue have been found to be the most serious reasons why applicants fail to do their best on civil service tests. Here is a list of reminders:

- Begin your preparation early – Don't wait until the last minute to go scurrying around for books and materials or to find out what the position is all about.
- Prepare continuously – An hour a night for a week is better than an all-night cram session. This has been definitely established. What is more, a night a week for a month will return better dividends than crowding your study into a shorter period of time.
- Locate the place of the exam – You have been sent a notice telling you when and where to report for the examination. If the location is in a different town or otherwise unfamiliar to you, it would be well to inquire the best route and learn something about the building.
- Relax the night before the test – Allow your mind to rest. Do not study at all that night. Plan some mild recreation or diversion; then go to bed early and get a good night's sleep.
- Get up early enough to make a leisurely trip to the place for the test – This way unforeseen events, traffic snarls, unfamiliar buildings, etc. will not upset you.
- Dress comfortably – A written test is not a fashion show. You will be known by number and not by name, so wear something comfortable.

- Leave excess paraphernalia at home – Shopping bags and odd bundles will get in your way. You need bring only the items mentioned in the official notice you received; usually everything you need is provided. Do not bring reference books to the exam. They will only confuse those last minutes and be taken away from you when in the test room.
- Arrive somewhat ahead of time – If because of transportation schedules you must get there very early, bring a newspaper or magazine to take your mind off yourself while waiting.
- Locate the examination room – When you have found the proper room, you will be directed to the seat or part of the room where you will sit. Sometimes you are given a sheet of instructions to read while you are waiting. Do not fill out any forms until you are told to do so; just read them and be prepared.
- Relax and prepare to listen to the instructions
- If you have any physical problem that may keep you from doing your best, be sure to tell the test administrator. If you are sick or in poor health, you really cannot do your best on the exam. You can come back and take the test some other time.

VII. AT THE TEST

The day of the test is here and you have the test booklet in your hand. The temptation to get going is very strong. Caution! There is more to success than knowing the right answers. You must know how to identify your papers and understand variations in the type of short-answer question used in this particular examination. Follow these suggestions for maximum results from your efforts:

1) Cooperate with the monitor

The test administrator has a duty to create a situation in which you can be as much at ease as possible. He will give instructions, tell you when to begin, check to see that you are marking your answer sheet correctly, and so on. He is not there to guard you, although he will see that your competitors do not take unfair advantage. He wants to help you do your best.

2) Listen to all instructions

Don't jump the gun! Wait until you understand all directions. In most civil service tests you get more time than you need to answer the questions. So don't be in a hurry. Read each word of instructions until you clearly understand the meaning. Study the examples, listen to all announcements and follow directions. Ask questions if you do not understand what to do.

3) Identify your papers

Civil service exams are usually identified by number only. You will be assigned a number; you must not put your name on your test papers. Be sure to copy your number correctly. Since more than one exam may be given, copy your exact examination title.

4) Plan your time

Unless you are told that a test is a "speed" or "rate of work" test, speed itself is usually not important. Time enough to answer all the questions will be provided, but this does not mean that you have all day. An overall time limit has been set. Divide the total time (in minutes) by the number of questions to determine the approximate time you have for each question.

5) Do not linger over difficult questions

If you come across a difficult question, mark it with a paper clip (useful to have along) and come back to it when you have been through the booklet. One caution if you do this – be sure to skip a number on your answer sheet as well. Check often to be sure that you have not lost your place and that you are marking in the row numbered the same as the question you are answering.

6) Read the questions

Be sure you know what the question asks! Many capable people are unsuccessful because they failed to *read* the questions correctly.

7) Answer all questions

Unless you have been instructed that a penalty will be deducted for incorrect answers, it is better to guess than to omit a question.

8) Speed tests

It is often better NOT to guess on speed tests. It has been found that on timed tests people are tempted to spend the last few seconds before time is called in marking answers at random – without even reading them – in the hope of picking up a few extra points. To discourage this practice, the instructions may warn you that your score will be "corrected" for guessing. That is, a penalty will be applied. The incorrect answers will be deducted from the correct ones, or some other penalty formula will be used.

9) Review your answers

If you finish before time is called, go back to the questions you guessed or omitted to give them further thought. Review other answers if you have time.

10) Return your test materials

If you are ready to leave before others have finished or time is called, take ALL your materials to the monitor and leave quietly. Never take any test material with you. The monitor can discover whose papers are not complete, and taking a test booklet may be grounds for disqualification.

VIII. EXAMINATION TECHNIQUES

1) Read the general instructions carefully. These are usually printed on the first page of the exam booklet. As a rule, these instructions refer to the timing of the examination; the fact that you should not start work until the signal and must stop work at a signal, etc. If there are any *special* instructions, such as a choice of questions to be answered, make sure that you note this instruction carefully.

2) When you are ready to start work on the examination, that is as soon as the signal has been given, read the instructions to each question booklet, underline any key words or phrases, such as *least, best, outline, describe* and the like. In this way you will tend to answer as requested rather than discover on reviewing your paper that you *listed without describing*, that you selected the *worst* choice rather than the *best* choice, etc.

3) If the examination is of the objective or multiple-choice type – that is, each question will also give a series of possible answers: A, B, C or D, and you are called upon to select the best answer and write the letter next to that answer on your answer paper – it is advisable to start answering each question in turn. There may be anywhere from 50 to 100 such questions in the three or four hours allotted and you can see how much time would be taken if you read through all the questions before beginning to answer any. Furthermore, if you come across a question or group of questions which you know would be difficult to answer, it would undoubtedly affect your handling of all the other questions.

4) If the examination is of the essay type and contains but a few questions, it is a moot point as to whether you should read all the questions before starting to answer any one. Of course, if you are given a choice – say five out of seven and the like – then it is essential to read all the questions so you can eliminate the two that are most difficult. If, however, you are asked to answer all the questions, there may be danger in trying to answer the easiest one first because you may find that you will spend too much time on it. The best technique is to answer the first question, then proceed to the second, etc.

5) Time your answers. Before the exam begins, write down the time it started, then add the time allowed for the examination and write down the time it must be completed, then divide the time available somewhat as follows:
    - If 3-1/2 hours are allowed, that would be 210 minutes. If you have 80 objective-type questions, that would be an average of 2-1/2 minutes per question. Allow yourself no more than 2 minutes per question, or a total of 160 minutes, which will permit about 50 minutes to review.
    - If for the time allotment of 210 minutes there are 7 essay questions to answer, that would average about 30 minutes a question. Give yourself only 25 minutes per question so that you have about 35 minutes to review.

6) The most important instruction is to *read each question* and make sure you know what is wanted. The second most important instruction is to *time yourself properly* so that you answer every question. The third most important instruction is to *answer every question*. Guess if you have to but include something for each question. Remember that you will receive no credit for a blank and will probably receive some credit if you write something in answer to an essay question. If you guess a letter – say "B" for a multiple-choice question – you may have guessed right. If you leave a blank as an answer to a multiple-choice question, the examiners may respect your feelings but it will not add a point to your score. Some exams may penalize you for wrong answers, so in such cases *only*, you may not want to guess unless you have some basis for your answer.

7) Suggestions
   a. Objective-type questions
      1. Examine the question booklet for proper sequence of pages and questions
      2. Read all instructions carefully
      3. Skip any question which seems too difficult; return to it after all other questions have been answered
      4. Apportion your time properly; do not spend too much time on any single question or group of questions

5. Note and underline key words – *all, most, fewest, least, best, worst, same, opposite,* etc.
6. Pay particular attention to negatives
7. Note unusual option, e.g., unduly long, short, complex, different or similar in content to the body of the question
8. Observe the use of "hedging" words – *probably, may, most likely,* etc.
9. Make sure that your answer is put next to the same number as the question
10. Do not second-guess unless you have good reason to believe the second answer is definitely more correct
11. Cross out original answer if you decide another answer is more accurate; do not erase until you are ready to hand your paper in
12. Answer all questions; guess unless instructed otherwise
13. Leave time for review

b. Essay questions
1. Read each question carefully
2. Determine exactly what is wanted. Underline key words or phrases.
3. Decide on outline or paragraph answer
4. Include many different points and elements unless asked to develop any one or two points or elements
5. Show impartiality by giving pros and cons unless directed to select one side only
6. Make and write down any assumptions you find necessary to answer the questions
7. Watch your English, grammar, punctuation and choice of words
8. Time your answers; don't crowd material

8) Answering the essay question

Most essay questions can be answered by framing the specific response around several key words or ideas. Here are a few such key words or ideas:

M's: manpower, materials, methods, money, management
P's: purpose, program, policy, plan, procedure, practice, problems, pitfalls, personnel, public relations

a. Six basic steps in handling problems:
1. Preliminary plan and background development
2. Collect information, data and facts
3. Analyze and interpret information, data and facts
4. Analyze and develop solutions as well as make recommendations
5. Prepare report and sell recommendations
6. Install recommendations and follow up effectiveness

b. Pitfalls to avoid
1. *Taking things for granted* – A statement of the situation does not necessarily imply that each of the elements is necessarily true; for example, a complaint may be invalid and biased so that all that can be taken for granted is that a complaint has been registered

2. *Considering only one side of a situation* – Wherever possible, indicate several alternatives and then point out the reasons you selected the best one
3. *Failing to indicate follow up* – Whenever your answer indicates action on your part, make certain that you will take proper follow-up action to see how successful your recommendations, procedures or actions turn out to be
4. *Taking too long in answering any single question* – Remember to time your answers properly

IX. AFTER THE TEST

Scoring procedures differ in detail among civil service jurisdictions although the general principles are the same. Whether the papers are hand-scored or graded by machine we have described, they are nearly always graded by number. That is, the person who marks the paper knows only the number – never the name – of the applicant. Not until all the papers have been graded will they be matched with names. If other tests, such as training and experience or oral interview ratings have been given, scores will be combined. Different parts of the examination usually have different weights. For example, the written test might count 60 percent of the final grade, and a rating of training and experience 40 percent. In many jurisdictions, veterans will have a certain number of points added to their grades.

After the final grade has been determined, the names are placed in grade order and an eligible list is established. There are various methods for resolving ties between those who get the same final grade – probably the most common is to place first the name of the person whose application was received first. Job offers are made from the eligible list in the order the names appear on it. You will be notified of your grade and your rank as soon as all these computations have been made. This will be done as rapidly as possible.

People who are found to meet the requirements in the announcement are called "eligibles." Their names are put on a list of eligible candidates. An eligible's chances of getting a job depend on how high he stands on this list and how fast agencies are filling jobs from the list.

When a job is to be filled from a list of eligibles, the agency asks for the names of people on the list of eligibles for that job. When the civil service commission receives this request, it sends to the agency the names of the three people highest on this list. Or, if the job to be filled has specialized requirements, the office sends the agency the names of the top three persons who meet these requirements from the general list.

The appointing officer makes a choice from among the three people whose names were sent to him. If the selected person accepts the appointment, the names of the others are put back on the list to be considered for future openings.

That is the rule in hiring from all kinds of eligible lists, whether they are for typist, carpenter, chemist, or something else. For every vacancy, the appointing officer has his choice of any one of the top three eligibles on the list. This explains why the person whose name is on top of the list sometimes does not get an appointment when some of the persons lower on the list do. If the appointing officer chooses the second or third eligible, the No. 1 eligible does not get a job at once, but stays on the list until he is appointed or the list is terminated.

X. HOW TO PASS THE INTERVIEW TEST

The examination for which you applied requires an oral interview test. You have already taken the written test and you are now being called for the interview test – the final part of the formal examination.

You may think that it is not possible to prepare for an interview test and that there are no procedures to follow during an interview. Our purpose is to point out some things you can do in advance that will help you and some good rules to follow and pitfalls to avoid while you are being interviewed.

What is an interview supposed to test?

The written examination is designed to test the technical knowledge and competence of the candidate; the oral is designed to evaluate intangible qualities, not readily measured otherwise, and to establish a list showing the relative fitness of each candidate – as measured against his competitors – for the position sought. Scoring is not on the basis of "right" and "wrong," but on a sliding scale of values ranging from "not passable" to "outstanding." As a matter of fact, it is possible to achieve a relatively low score without a single "incorrect" answer because of evident weakness in the qualities being measured.

Occasionally, an examination may consist entirely of an oral test – either an individual or a group oral. In such cases, information is sought concerning the technical knowledges and abilities of the candidate, since there has been no written examination for this purpose. More commonly, however, an oral test is used to supplement a written examination.

Who conducts interviews?

The composition of oral boards varies among different jurisdictions. In nearly all, a representative of the personnel department serves as chairman. One of the members of the board may be a representative of the department in which the candidate would work. In some cases, "outside experts" are used, and, frequently, a businessman or some other representative of the general public is asked to serve. Labor and management or other special groups may be represented. The aim is to secure the services of experts in the appropriate field.

However the board is composed, it is a good idea (and not at all improper or unethical) to ascertain in advance of the interview who the members are and what groups they represent. When you are introduced to them, you will have some idea of their backgrounds and interests, and at least you will not stutter and stammer over their names.

What should be done before the interview?

While knowledge about the board members is useful and takes some of the surprise element out of the interview, there is other preparation which is more substantive. It *is* possible to prepare for an oral interview – in several ways:

1) Keep a copy of your application and review it carefully before the interview

This may be the only document before the oral board, and the starting point of the interview. Know what education and experience you have listed there, and the sequence and dates of all of it. Sometimes the board will ask you to review the highlights of your experience for them; you should not have to hem and haw doing it.

2) Study the class specification and the examination announcement

Usually, the oral board has one or both of these to guide them. The qualities, characteristics or knowledges required by the position sought are stated in these documents. They offer valuable clues as to the nature of the oral interview. For example, if the job involves supervisory responsibilities, the announcement will usually indicate that knowledge of modern supervisory methods and the qualifications of the candidate as a supervisor will be tested. If so, you can expect such questions, frequently in the form of a hypothetical situation which you are expected to solve. NEVER go into an oral without knowledge of the duties and responsibilities of the job you seek.

3) Think through each qualification required

Try to visualize the kind of questions you would ask if you were a board member. How well could you answer them? Try especially to appraise your own knowledge and background in each area, *measured against the job sought*, and identify any areas in which you are weak. Be critical and realistic – do not flatter yourself.

4) Do some general reading in areas in which you feel you may be weak

For example, if the job involves supervision and your past experience has NOT, some general reading in supervisory methods and practices, particularly in the field of human relations, might be useful. Do NOT study agency procedures or detailed manuals. The oral board will be testing your understanding and capacity, not your memory.

5) Get a good night's sleep and watch your general health and mental attitude

You will want a clear head at the interview. Take care of a cold or any other minor ailment, and of course, no hangovers.

What should be done on the day of the interview?

Now comes the day of the interview itself. Give yourself plenty of time to get there. Plan to arrive somewhat ahead of the scheduled time, particularly if your appointment is in the fore part of the day. If a previous candidate fails to appear, the board might be ready for you a bit early. By early afternoon an oral board is almost invariably behind schedule if there are many candidates, and you may have to wait. Take along a book or magazine to read, or your application to review, but leave any extraneous material in the waiting room when you go in for your interview. In any event, relax and compose yourself.

The matter of dress is important. The board is forming impressions about you – from your experience, your manners, your attitude, and your appearance. Give your personal appearance careful attention. Dress your best, but not your flashiest. Choose conservative, appropriate clothing, and be sure it is immaculate. This is a business interview, and your appearance should indicate that you regard it as such. Besides, being well groomed and properly dressed will help boost your confidence.

Sooner or later, someone will call your name and escort you into the interview room. *This is it.* From here on you are on your own. It is too late for any more preparation. But remember, you asked for this opportunity to prove your fitness, and you are here because your request was granted.

What happens when you go in?

The usual sequence of events will be as follows: The clerk (who is often the board stenographer) will introduce you to the chairman of the oral board, who will introduce you to the other members of the board. Acknowledge the introductions before you sit down. Do not be surprised if you find a microphone facing you or a stenotypist sitting by. Oral interviews are usually recorded in the event of an appeal or other review.

Usually the chairman of the board will open the interview by reviewing the highlights of your education and work experience from your application – primarily for the benefit of the other members of the board, as well as to get the material into the record. Do not interrupt or comment unless there is an error or significant misinterpretation; if that is the case, do not hesitate. But do not quibble about insignificant matters. Also, he will usually ask you some question about your education, experience or your present job – partly to get you to start talking and to establish the interviewing "rapport." He may start the actual questioning, or turn it over to one of the other members. Frequently, each member undertakes the questioning on a particular area, one in which he is perhaps most competent, so you can expect each member to participate in the examination. Because time is limited, you may also expect some rather abrupt switches in the direction the questioning takes, so do not be upset by it. Normally, a board member will not pursue a single line of questioning unless he discovers a particular strength or weakness.

After each member has participated, the chairman will usually ask whether any member has any further questions, then will ask you if you have anything you wish to add. Unless you are expecting this question, it may floor you. Worse, it may start you off on an extended, extemporaneous speech. The board is not usually seeking more information. The question is principally to offer you a last opportunity to present further qualifications or to indicate that you have nothing to add. So, if you feel that a significant qualification or characteristic has been overlooked, it is proper to point it out in a sentence or so. Do not compliment the board on the thoroughness of their examination – they have been sketchy, and you know it. If you wish, merely say, "No thank you, I have nothing further to add." This is a point where you can "talk yourself out" of a good impression or fail to present an important bit of information. Remember, *you close the interview yourself.*

The chairman will then say, "That is all, Mr. _____, thank you." Do not be startled; the interview is over, and quicker than you think. Thank him, gather your belongings and take your leave. Save your sigh of relief for the other side of the door.

How to put your best foot forward

Throughout this entire process, you may feel that the board individually and collectively is trying to pierce your defenses, seek out your hidden weaknesses and embarrass and confuse you. Actually, this is not true. They are obliged to make an appraisal of your qualifications for the job you are seeking, and they want to see you in your best light. Remember, they must interview all candidates and a non-cooperative candidate may become a failure in spite of their best efforts to bring out his qualifications. Here are 15 suggestions that will help you:

1) Be natural – Keep your attitude confident, not cocky

If you are not confident that you can do the job, do not expect the board to be. Do not apologize for your weaknesses, try to bring out your strong points. The board is interested in a positive, not negative, presentation. Cockiness will antagonize any board member and make him wonder if you are covering up a weakness by a false show of strength.

2) Get comfortable, but don't lounge or sprawl

Sit erectly but not stiffly. A careless posture may lead the board to conclude that you are careless in other things, or at least that you are not impressed by the importance of the occasion. Either conclusion is natural, even if incorrect. Do not fuss with your clothing, a pencil or an ashtray. Your hands may occasionally be useful to emphasize a point; do not let them become a point of distraction.

3) Do not wisecrack or make small talk

This is a serious situation, and your attitude should show that you consider it as such. Further, the time of the board is limited – they do not want to waste it, and neither should you.

4) Do not exaggerate your experience or abilities

In the first place, from information in the application or other interviews and sources, the board may know more about you than you think. Secondly, you probably will not get away with it. An experienced board is rather adept at spotting such a situation, so do not take the chance.

5) If you know a board member, do not make a point of it, yet do not hide it

Certainly you are not fooling him, and probably not the other members of the board. Do not try to take advantage of your acquaintanceship – it will probably do you little good.

6) Do not dominate the interview

Let the board do that. They will give you the clues – do not assume that you have to do all the talking. Realize that the board has a number of questions to ask you, and do not try to take up all the interview time by showing off your extensive knowledge of the answer to the first one.

7) Be attentive

You only have 20 minutes or so, and you should keep your attention at its sharpest throughout. When a member is addressing a problem or question to you, give him your undivided attention. Address your reply principally to him, but do not exclude the other board members.

8) Do not interrupt

A board member may be stating a problem for you to analyze. He will ask you a question when the time comes. Let him state the problem, and wait for the question.

9) Make sure you understand the question

Do not try to answer until you are sure what the question is. If it is not clear, restate it in your own words or ask the board member to clarify it for you. However, do not haggle about minor elements.

10) Reply promptly but not hastily

A common entry on oral board rating sheets is "candidate responded readily," or "candidate hesitated in replies." Respond as promptly and quickly as you can, but do not jump to a hasty, ill-considered answer.

11) Do not be peremptory in your answers

A brief answer is proper – but do not fire your answer back. That is a losing game from your point of view. The board member can probably ask questions much faster than you can answer them.

12) Do not try to create the answer you think the board member wants

He is interested in what kind of mind you have and how it works – not in playing games. Furthermore, he can usually spot this practice and will actually grade you down on it.

13) Do not switch sides in your reply merely to agree with a board member

Frequently, a member will take a contrary position merely to draw you out and to see if you are willing and able to defend your point of view. Do not start a debate, yet do not surrender a good position. If a position is worth taking, it is worth defending.

14) Do not be afraid to admit an error in judgment if you are shown to be wrong

The board knows that you are forced to reply without any opportunity for careful consideration. Your answer may be demonstrably wrong. If so, admit it and get on with the interview.

15) Do not dwell at length on your present job

The opening question may relate to your present assignment. Answer the question but do not go into an extended discussion. You are being examined for a *new* job, not your present one. As a matter of fact, try to phrase ALL your answers in terms of the job for which you are being examined.

Basis of Rating

Probably you will forget most of these "do's" and "don'ts" when you walk into the oral interview room. Even remembering them all will not ensure you a passing grade. Perhaps you did not have the qualifications in the first place. But remembering them will help you to put your best foot forward, without treading on the toes of the board members.

Rumor and popular opinion to the contrary notwithstanding, an oral board wants you to make the best appearance possible. They know you are under pressure – but they also want to see how you respond to it as a guide to what your reaction would be under the pressures of the job you seek. They will be influenced by the degree of poise you display, the personal traits you show and the manner in which you respond.

ABOUT THIS BOOK

This book contains tests divided into Examination Sections. Go through each test, answering every question in the margin. We have also attached a sample answer sheet at the back of the book that can be removed and used. At the end of each test look at the answer key and check your answers. On the ones you got wrong, look at the right answer choice and learn. Do not fill in the answers first. Do not memorize the questions and answers, but understand the answer and principles involved. On your test, the questions will likely be different from the samples. Questions are changed and new ones added. If you understand these past questions you should have success with any changes that arise. Tests may consist of several types of questions. We have additional books on each subject should more study be advisable or necessary for you. Finally, the more you study, the better prepared you will be. This book is intended to be the last thing you study before you walk into the examination room. Prior study of relevant texts is also recommended. NLC publishes some of these in our Fundamental Series. Knowledge and good sense are important factors in passing your exam. Good luck also helps. So now study this Passbook, absorb the material contained within and take that knowledge into the examination. Then do your best to pass that exam.

EXAMINATION SECTION

EXAMINATION SECTION
TEST 1

DIRECTIONS: Each question or incomplete statement is followed by several suggested answers or completions. Select the one that BEST answers the question or completes the statement. PRINT THE LETTER OF THE CORRECT ANSWER IN THE SPACE AT THE RIGHT.

1. The recreation leader is tasked with researching and developing 1._____
    A. quality sport and recreation
    B. recreation and leisure programs
    C. quality sport, recreation and leisure programs
    D. quality sport and leisure programs

2. One of the main responsibilities for a recreation leader in terms of interacting 2._____
with the public is
    A. teaching about the importance and history of recreation programs
    B. officiating games and enforcing rules
    C. maintaining comfortable conditions in facility buildings
    D. informing about programs available to the community

3. Which of these would NOT be considered a responsibility of the recreational 3._____
leader?
    A. Develop and/or preserve recreation/sport programs
    B. Ensure recreation information is available for all who want it
    C. Supervise other staff members to make sure they are pulling their weight
    D. Appraise the effectiveness of current programs

4. What is the insurance type that covers any liability that is a direct result from 4._____
damage to property, and death/injury because of negligence?
    A. Motor vehicle liability
    B. Property liability
    C. Public liability
    D. Indemnity liability

5. Which of the following is an important personal trait for a recreational leader? 5._____
    A. Highly skilled at sports
    B. Flexibility
    C. Strict enforcement of all administrative and sports rules at all times
    D. Pressuring community members to join programs

6. Which of the following is NOT a skill that the recreational leader must exhibit? 6._____
    A. Problem solving
    B. Effective verbal and listening communication
    C. Time management
    D. Humor

7. Which of the following would be considered a physical demand of recreational leaders?
   A. Lifting, carrying and managing equipment and supplies
   B. Juggling multiple requests and projects at one time
   C. Using a computer/laptop to set up program dates and/or print out flyers
   D. Busy/noisy environments

7._____

8. The most common working places for people working in the recreational field are
   A. community centers
   B. gymnasiums
   C. youth camps
   D. all of the above

8._____

9. Money gained from entry fees was not enough to pay for your facility's yearly Fun Run 5k. In order to ensure it does not happen again next year, what funding source would be best for helping with the extra costs of operating the Fun Run?
   A. Charities
   B. Higher entry fees
   C. Grants from local government
   D. Commercial/business sponsorships

9._____

10. As a recreational assistant, you have been tasked with putting up "How To" posters around the workout facility. Which of the following would be the most effective message regarding proper posture during sports or weightlifting?
    A. "In order to properly ensure you stand with your back in the proper position, put your ears, shoulders and hips in a straight line."
    B. "Flex your spine when you stand to make sure your back and neck are in line."
    C. "When standing, make sure your weight is toward the back of your body; this will decrease the weight load at the front."
    D. "Extend your upper torso forward slightly; this will help you stand the right way."

10._____

11. The job functions of a recreation worker include
    A. scheduling activities
    B. distributing and maintaining control of equipment/supplies
    C. participating in programs that they create
    D. both A and B

11._____

12. What is the approximate weight of a 5-gallon jug of Gatorade?
    A. 20 quarts
    B. 40 ounces
    C. 40 pounds
    D. 100 pounds

12._____

13. A recreation leader's knowledge of common sports and games is   13._____
    A. not important, as long as they are effective at other duties
    B. somewhat important; more knowledgeable assistants will be responsible for the finer details
    C. very important; it's the leader's job to have a strong understanding of the programs he or she is creating
    D. only important if they are under the age of 25

14. Of the following examples, which one best demonstrates an effective recreational leader?   14._____
    A. Moderate attendance of programs
    B. Employees under the leader complaining about program efficiency
    C. Campers returning to programs year after year
    D. Constant community awareness of new and updated programs and events

15. As a sports and recreational employee, which of the following is NOT an acceptable instruction method?   15._____
    A. Being approachable
    B. Being critical and discouraging
    C. Motivating everyone to do their best
    D. Having an organized and efficient plan

16. You have been tasked with recording campers' mile-run times and printing them in a chart from fastest to slowest, with results to be posted in the gym. The BEST computer program to use for this type of work is   16._____
    A. Microsoft Excel
    B. Microsoft Word
    C. Microsoft PowerPoint
    D. Adobe Acrobat

17. A camper asks for a guideline to incorporate into his health and wellness plan. He is moderately fit and enjoys the outdoors (biking, hiking, jogging, etc.). What is the most appropriate plan for him to follow to start with?   17._____
    A. His exercise intensity should make his heart rate raise to about 70% of his max heart rate
    B. Work out for about 20 minutes three times per week
    C. His exercise intensity should make his heart rate raise to about 85% of his max heart rate
    D. Work out for about 90 minutes each day of the week

18. What attributes are given to a recreational leader or assistant based on his/her coaching style, how he/she communicates, teaches and motivates?   18._____
    A. Credibility
    B. Respect
    C. Trust
    D. All of the above

19. Which of the following is a legal duty of anyone involved in recreational sports management?
    A. They must properly instruct techniques
    B. Participants need to be warned of the natural dangers of the sport/activity
    C. The rec leaders must be able to anticipate potential problems or dangers
    D. There must be a constant monitoring of a participant's development

19._____

20. Safety education programs may include which of the following in the recreational industry environment?
    A. Enforcement of rules
    B. Restriction of access to facilities
    C. Workplace inspection
    D. Signs, films and presentations

20._____

21. When someone goes through long periods of exercising without drinking water to rehydrate, loss of fluids because of sweating could lead to
    A. a lower heart rate
    B. body temperature cooler than average
    C. a reduction of blood plasma
    D. none of the above

21._____

22. While overseeing participants involved in a weightlifting program at one of your facilities, you notice a few teenage boys lifting with weighted bars and dumbbells faster than is safe and with jerky movements. When you explain to them why they should avoid lifting in this manner, what do these speedy and jerky movements force them to do?
    A. They make their backs pull into an upright position, when it should be arched during the lift
    B. They are drastically increasing the pressure placed on their spine and spinal muscles
    C. They cause their side to bend and twist resulting in flexing muscles laterally
    D. They are mostly using their own momentum, which means their muscles are hardly doing any work

22._____

23. Which of the following has been an essential development in the growth of leisure and recreation programs?
    A. The surge in free time during the latter part of the 20th century
    B. A population that is rapidly aging
    C. The increase in family income
    D. The smaller family size starting from WWII

23._____

24. Studies have revealed that recreational fitness programs that are found to be successful usually include all of the following EXCEPT
    A. personal satisfaction
    B. a format that allows enjoyment of the activity
    C. cardiovascular training
    D. recreational interest

25. One misconception of organizing and executing leisure programs is
    A. it is something that can be done by anyone who is willing to put up with the role
    B. it is not worthy of dollars or government interest
    C. it is a relatively simple task that the average person can do with a familiarity and understanding of sports
    D. state and federal agencies should be primarily responsible for it

---

KEY (CORRECT ANSWERS)

1. C	11. D
2. D	12. C
3. C	13. C
4. D	14. D
5. B	15. B
6. D	16. A
7. A	17. A
8. D	18. D
9. D	19. A
10. A	20. D

21. C
22. B
23. A
24. C
25. C

TEST 2

DIRECTIONS: Each question or incomplete statement is followed by several suggested answers or completions. Select the one that BEST answers the question or completes the statement. PRINT THE LETTER OF THE CORRECT ANSWER IN THE SPACE AT THE RIGHT.

1. A participant in one of your programs has filled out that she is severely allergic to bee stings, which would typically cause
    a. septic shock
    b. anaphylactic shock
    c. toxic shock syndrome
    d. cardiac arrest

    1._____

2. If group morale is low, a recreational leader should
    a. intermittently divide into subgroups
    b. ignore the situation, as the group will work through it
    c. adjust group goals to better echo the needs of each individual
    d. change to a more overbearing leadership style

    2._____

3. Which of the following is a hindrance to, rather than a result of, effective group decision-making?
    a. Information exchange
    b. Variety of individual motives
    c. Increased acceptance of decisions
    d. Security in making tough decisions

    3._____

4. A common injury associated with play and sports on artificial turf is
    a. sore shoulder
    b. elbow and knee friction burns
    c. strained hamstring
    d. bruising

    4._____

5. A common injury associated with uneven playing surfaces (i.e. soccer fields, baseball diamonds) is
    a. athlete's foot
    b. bone bruise
    c. heel soreness
    d. sprained ankle

    5._____

6. If you come across a camper whose life-threatening condition involves the inability to breathe, what treatment should you use?
    a. The Heimlich Maneuver, two rescue breaths and CPR
    b. Start CPR immediately
    c. Twelve to fifteen rescue breaths per minute and correct CPR
    d. You should follow the steps for rescue breathing

    6._____

7. Expectations of park and recreation leaders are that they should perform   7._____
    a. effectively
    b. efficiently
    c. both efficiently and effectively
    d. more effectively than efficiently

8. To draw a bearing of 240 degrees on a map, which of the following steps apply?   8._____
    a. Set the compass to north
    b. Orient the map to magnetic north
    c. Set the compass to 240 degrees
    d. Draw a line along the edge of the compass

9. One of the children at your youth summer camp sprained his ankle during an activity. What is the proper way to treat his injury?   9._____
    a. Do not remove the shoe; put on an ankle bandage for support, then elevate the ankle and wrap it in cold towels/ice
    b. Take the shoe off and rotate the foot, checking for swelling
    c. Have the child keep his shoe on, apply an ankle splint and wrap the ankle in a heated towel
    d. Tell the camper to "walk it off" in order prevent stiffness from setting in

10. Which of the following correctly pairs the sport and a basic piece of equipment used during play?   10._____
    a. Baseball; stick
    b. Golf; driver
    c. Badminton; puck
    d. Football; boot

11. During a baseball game you notice that an 11-year-old boy is throwing curveballs. You tell him to stop immediately because   11._____
    a. the other campers are complaining
    b. he's having better success with his fastball
    c. he needs permission from his Little League coach to throw breaking pitches
    d. this puts an unhealthy strain on his arm and could lead to permanent elbow and shoulder problems

12. Which of the following are required safety items for soccer games?   12._____
    a. Shorts
    b. Knee pads
    c. Helmets
    d. Shin guards

13. Leisure education is
    a. Learning to value and prioritize leisure in life
    b. A concept that is increasingly less valid in modern-day recreation
    c. Taking time to relax for a short period of time
    d. A and C only

13._____

14. A parent called you to complain that one of your staff members did not treat their child's poison ivy rash properly. When you talk to the staff member, what should you tell them about how to properly treat poison ivy?
    a. Don't do anything for 20 minutes, then wash the area with hot water and soap
    b. Rinse off the area as soon as possible with soapy water
    c. Tell the child to continue wearing his/her clothes that have had contact with plants
    d. Immediately cover the exposed area with calamine lotion

14._____

15. Which term is commonly associated with the end of a tennis match?
    a. Match point
    b. Set point
    c. Break point
    d. Ace

15._____

16. Which term is commonly associated with a tennis serve?
    a. Ace
    b. Let
    c. Fault
    d. All of the above

16._____

17. A recreational instructor has a variety of duties, and chief among them is a moral obligation to
    a. create an atmosphere absent of discrimination
    b. ensure participants' level of education increases
    c. continue to update members' records of home addresses
    d. provide constant updates on attendance of participants

17._____

18. The gymnasium lights tend to get extremely warm during the day because of the halogen lights currently installed. Which of the following would be a good replacement in order to avoid overheating or busted lights?
    a. LED
    b. Keep halogen lights
    c. Incandescent
    d. None of the above

18._____

19. Which of the following is considered poor technique when shooting free throws in a basketball game?   19._____
    a. Bent knees
    b. Pre-shot dribbles
    c. Bent elbows
    d. Jumping

20. The most appropriate basketball drills for a group of 8- and 9-year-old campers would involve   20._____
    a. zone and trap defenses
    b. three-point shots
    c. chest and bounce passes
    d. screens and skip passes

21. Teenagers who possess high self-esteem are more likely to take part in   21._____
    a. team sports and/or musical groups
    b. outdoor recreation
    c. both A and B
    d. none of the above

22. One of the reasons people advocate leisure and recreation is because it keeps which group from being overly influenced by movies, television, mass media and music?   22._____
    a. The general public
    b. Toddlers
    c. Middle-aged adults
    d. Teenagers

23. Which of the following best defines "workaholism"?   23._____
    a. Being unable to choose an enticing career
    b. The inability to focus on one's job
    c. Expectations so high from employers that it is impossible to measure up to
    d. An obsessive need to work and the inability to find happiness in other activities

24. Before 1974, girls were not allowed to participate in   24._____
    a. Little League
    b. Cub Scouts
    c. Pop Warner football
    d. none of the above

25. Which of the following terms refers to a significant clustering of people with a common bond?   25._____
    a. Social agency
    b. Town
    c. Locale
    d. Neighborhood

KEY (CORRECT ANSWERS)

1. B
2. C
3. B
4. B
5. D

6. A
7. C
8. B
9. A
10. B

11. D
12. D
13. D
14. B
15. A

16. D
17. A
18. A
19. D
20. C

21. C
22. D
23. D
24. A
25. D

TEST 3

DIRECTIONS: Each question or incomplete statement is followed by several suggested answers or completions. Select the one that BEST answers the question or completes the statement. PRINT THE LETTER OF THE CORRECT ANSWER IN THE SPACE AT THE RIGHT.

1. As a recreational leader, it is important to integrate disabled participants into programs with non-disabled participants.
   This important concept is better known as
   a. segregation
   b. mainstreaming
   c. separate but equal
   d. all of the above

   1._____

2. Which of the following terms does NOT apply to golf?
   a. Spar
   b. Birdie
   c. Wedge
   d. Stroke

   2._____

3. Sports offer many social values including all of the following EXCEPT
   a. learning to obey rules
   b. the importance of winning
   c. allowing opportunity for social mobility
   d. a dedication to team-based goals

   3._____

4. As a recreational supervisor, it is important to develop a document that outlines his/her agency's direction and overall goals and objectives. This is usually known as a(n)
   a. manifesto
   b. directive
   c. mission statement
   d. order

   4._____

5. Risk management is a part of recreational activities. Which of the following measures are important to incorporate into programs to ensure proper risk management steps have been taken?
   a. Yearly staff training to ensure skills and knowledge are current
   b. Staff goes through specific technical qualifications for "high risk" activities
   c. Both A and B
   d. None of the above

   5._____

6. Encouraging students to explore their natural environment is an important aspect of
   a. valuing nature and cultural heritage
   b. getting outside once in awhile
   c. exercising and becoming fit
   d. supporting stronger community cohesiveness

7. Which of the following is a great reason to promote recreational programs to youth?
   a. It will provide a chance to meet members of the opposite sex
   b. It stimulates the local economy by paying for various programs
   c. It allows parents to get a break from their children once in a while
   d. It encourages social interaction and teamwork

8. If you were to determine the cost of each camper in your youth program, you would need to divide
   a. total expenses by total campers signed up and paid
   b. all classes offered by how many were conducted
   c. the amount of successful programs by total registered campers
   d. the number of campers enrolled by the total number of programs

9. Proper maintenance of a baseball/softball field for ease of play, safety and longevity of the surface involves all of the following EXCEPT
   a. raking the infield and home plate area
   b. reseeding the outfield grass on a monthly basis
   c. lining the foul lines and batters box
   d. removing litter and debris in the infield and outfield

10. You are a recreational facility manager tasked with lowering the amount of serious injuries on a playground. The FIRST step you should take to carry out this initiative is to
    a. hold a meeting on proper maintenance of playing surfaces
    b. replace all old and outdated equipment
    c. ensure yearly safety inspections are carried out
    d. add more space between each piece of equipment

11. A deaf participant has signed up to take part in a mountain hike offered through your local parks and recreation building. If the deaf child's parent requested someone who could speak sign language to accompany them on the hike, how should your office respond?
    a. Inform the parent that they will need to provide their own sign language interpreter
    b. Call a local agency and hire someone who speaks sign language attend the hike and then send the bill to the family
    c. Tell the family to attend social activities for those who are deaf
    d. Contact a sign language interpreter and make arrangements for them to be on the hike

12. Of the following, what is the BEST reason for staff members to wear a uniform?
    a. It will improve the safety of staff and participants
    b. It makes buying and ordering merchandise so much easier
    c. It makes the staff image look better
    d. It allows the public to easily identify staff members

13. Which of the following techniques is good to keep in mind when teaching players to dribble a soccer ball?
    a. Kick the ball altering between both feet while keeping your eyes on the ball
    b. Move at a speed greater than walking and keep the ball within 2-4 feet of the body
    c. Run in a zigzag pattern and keep the ball right below your head while moving
    d. While running, deliver a series of taps to the ball with your foot

14. Assuming that volunteering to work special recreational events is an intrinsic motivation, what would be the most meaningful way to recognize the volunteers for their exemplary work performance?
    a. The ability to use facilities free of charge
    b. A small cash consideration with a thank you card
    c. At the following event, stand up and acknowledge the volunteers for their hard work
    d. Present a plaque for them at a formal ceremony

15. If you need to fill a moveable gasoline tank to take on a boating activity, how should you fill it up?
    a. On the pier
    b. On the boat
    c. By keeping the nozzle in contact with the tank's rim
    d. Both a and c

16. If you came into contact with a white buoy that had an orange diamond on it, that would mean
    a. safe water
    b. hazardous area
    c. you can go on either side of the buoy
    d. it doesn't mean anything

17. After engaging in an aerobic exercise, what is the normal physiological response?
    a. Heart rate increase and decrease in stroke volume
    b. Increase in consuming and ventilating dioxygen (O2)
    c. Decreasing of cardiac output
    d. Decrease of blood flow to muscles that are working

18. You have set up a weight-loss program at one of your facilities. If two people are the same weight and follow your program strictly, they will
    a. lose the exact same amount of weight during the program
    b. each have a different response to the program
    c. most likely eat the same amount of food each day
    d. put on the same amount of muscles

18._____

19. When teaching young participants how to throw a softball, what is the best way to instruct them?
    a. Tell them to release the ball at chest level
    b. Instruct them to stop the action of follow through right before releasing the ball
    c. Have the participants start their throws with the side of their body facing the target
    d. Participants should take one step forward with the foot opposite of the throwing hand

19._____

20. In a physical activity, participants in a youth program work together in pairs with a ball. The pairs start out close to each other, tossing the ball back and forth and then they gradually move farther and farther apart until they cannot successfully throw the ball to one another. Which of the following concepts is the lesson designed to teach?
    a. Speed
    b. Range
    c. Dealing with failure
    d. Passing skills

20._____

21. Which of the following is an important aspect of public recreation agencies?
    a. Gaining federal grants for playgrounds in underprivileged areas
    b. Ensuring that leisure and recreation is available in cities everywhere
    c. Promoting unity and cohesion between different racial/ethnic groups through leisure programs
    d. None of the above

21._____

22. Which of the following correctly pairs a sport and an infraction committed during gameplay?
    a. Bowling – strike
    b. Golf – bogey
    c. Football – tackle
    d. Soccer – handball

22._____

23. Not all leisure activities are considered playful or sporty. Which of the following choices is a good example of a non-play leisure activity? 23._____
    a. Working overtime
    b. Reading a novel
    c. Taking a test
    d. Cleaning

24. A recreation volunteer is asked to organize a game that requires only a ball and a net. All of the following can be played EXCEPT 24._____
    a. soccer
    b. European handball
    c. lacrosse
    d. volleyball

25. Which of the following would BEST describe a program that allows for support of disabled people? 25._____
    a. A water polo program with coaches making sure everyone plays by the rules
    b. A soccer program that puts vests on disabled participants so others won't hurt them
    c. A bowling program that has adaptive bowling equipment available at each lane
    d. A volleyball program that keeps the disabled and nondisabled participants separate

KEY (CORRECT ANSWERS)

1. B 11. D
2. A 12. D
3. B 13. A
4. C 14. C
5. C 15. D

6. A 16. B
7. D 17. A
8. A 18. B
9. B 19. D
10. B 20. B

21. C
22. D
23. B
24. C
25. C

TEST 4

DIRECTIONS: Each question or incomplete statement is followed by several suggested answers or completions. Select the one that BEST answers the question or completes the statement. PRINT THE LETTER OF THE CORRECT ANSWER IN THE SPACE AT THE RIGHT.

1. The YMCA was so successful in its early years because 1._____
    a. it combined with another youth association so they had greater numbers and support
    b. they specifically sought out individuals who had clear financial support
    c. the marketing department advertised to a wide variety of people
    d. they managed to cross religious, social and racial divides when attracting people to their facilities

2. Which of the following would be considered support for a disabled person in an activity? 2._____
    a. Making sure the disabled participant has use of adaptive devices/equipment
    b. Telling the participant to watch an instructional video before taking part in the activity
    c. Having them sit and watch while you play for them
    d. Tell the other participants to treat the disabled participant specially

3. Diversity within programs at your recreational facility refers to 3._____
    a. ensuring all activities have ethnically diverse groups
    b. creating and offering a vast amount of activities for participants of varying backgrounds, ethnicities and races
    c. having a variety of social and leisure activities for random people to engage in
    d. the amount of different activities that people will participate in over the course of their lives

4. Which of the following terms best define leisure? 4._____
    a. Learning
    b. Competing
    c. Community
    d. Freedom

5. One way of volunteering in recreational service would be to work for the Special Olympics. This organization serves people who 5._____
    a. have spine injuries
    b. are amputees
    c. have developmental disabilities
    d. all of the above

6. Which of the following is defined as an immediate, innately rewarding activity that requires very little to no special training to enjoy?
    a. The balance between work and leisure
    b. Physiological leisure
    c. Casual leisure
    d. Serious leisure

7. In a staff meeting, you outline the need to get which of the following groups away from television because it potentially causes them to become more aggressive and violent?
    a. Children
    b. Adolescent teens
    c. Adults
    d. Both A and B

8. A parent of a disabled child comes to you and states: "I don't want my child to try this new activity because I don't think he will be very successful with it." Which of the following statements would be the BEST way to respond?
    a. "Would you like him to explore alternative activities?"
    b. "How does HE feel about this activity?"
    c. "Why don't you let him try the activity?; Most people enjoy it."
    d. "Do you think that he lacks the skills to participate?"

9. You are overseeing an activity involving elementary-aged participants who are learning to play soccer. Some parents, despite you telling them they could leave, are 'hovering' and try to get involved. Which of the following is the term given to parents like this?
    a. Obsessive
    b. Helicopter
    c. Excessive
    d. Good and caring

10. The fact that a parks and recreational institute would provide community members with jobs, increase the value of the land in the area and would help people reduce their healthcare costs due to healthier lifestyle are all considered what types of benefits?
    a. Individual
    b. Economic
    c. Cultural
    d. None of the above

11. If you are choosing activities based on minimizing risk, which of the following should be avoided because it is the leading cause of accidents for youth participants?
    a. Soccer
    b. Swimming
    c. Bike riding
    d. Baseball/softball

12. The U.S. National Park Service includes
    a. historic battlefields
    b. volcanoes
    c. homesteads
    d. all of the above

    12._____

13. What year was the U.S. National Park Service created?
    a. 1955
    b. 1794
    c. 1916
    d. 1856

    13._____

14. A parent comes in complaining that his child wants to be involved with parks and recreation but doesn't want to do anything "sporty" or physical. Which of the following recommendations would be best for her child to participate in?
    a. Soccer
    b. Camping
    c. Mountain climbing
    d. Pottery

    14._____

15. A flat, wooden-backed brush with bristles would be best used to keep which of the following surfaces maintained?
    a. The gymnasium's windows
    b. The parking lot
    c. The toilets
    d. The gymnasium's floors

    15._____

16. A youth participant cuts his hand during one of your activities. One of your youth leaders is about to clean the cut but he doesn't put on gloves. You remind him that he should always wear gloves when cleaning out a wound in order to
    a. avoid catching a cold from them
    b. keep the hands from smelling like blood
    c. get a better grip on the wound
    d. protect against germs and infection

    16._____

17. If you are forced to make a 911 call, what are the 3 questions you must answer first when talking to the dispatcher?
    a. Who, What, Where
    b. Where, What and Why
    c. Why, When and Where
    d. Who, What and When

    17._____

18. To determine which programs are required, the recreation leader should
    a. ask a few community members what they want
    b. complete a needs assessment
    c. pick a few random programs to see if they work
    d. ask his/her boss what to do

19. Your supervisor has mandated that the Facility Manager Office needs to reduce building cooling costs. Which of the following would NOT be the recommended way to do that most effectively?
    a. Weatherstrip doors and windows
    b. Increase cool water flow in dishwashing systems
    c. Ensure adequate ventilation in attic spaces
    d. Close air supply and exhaust duct dampers when not in use

20. Your weekend program designed for at-risk kids has to be modified slightly because a number of staff members have called in sick. If youth participants typically rotate through a variety of activities, which of the following parts of the program planning will need to be changed?
    a. Goal-oriented programming
    b. Sequence of events and time frame
    c. Supply needs
    d. Client safety

21. When building indoor facilities, which of the following is built primarily to host sport and entertainment events?
    a. Theater
    b. Convention center
    c. Stadium
    d. Arena

22. Making a correct and fair decision is referred to as
    a. code of ethics
    b. morality
    c. immorality
    d. ethical dilemma

23. Which of the following would be an example of technical knowledge that a recreation leader would need to perform well at his or her job?
    a. How to create and send out an e-newsletter to the community
    b. How to peacefully resolve conflicts between activity participants
    c. How to strategically plan programs for an entire calendar year
    d. Both A and B

24. To become a Certified Park and Recreation Professional, you would take a certification test administered by
    a. NRPA
    b. NRA
    c. YMCA
    d. CPRP

25. Which president is credited with developing the National Parks system   25._____
    when he established Yellowstone in 1872?
    a. Theodore Roosevelt
    b. Abraham Lincoln
    c. Ulysses S. Grant
    d. Chester A. Arthur

KEY (CORRECT ANSWERS)

1. D
2. A
3. B
4. D
5. C

6. C
7. D
8. D
9. B
10. B

11. A
12. D
13. C
14. D
15. D

16. D
17. A
18. B
19. B
20. B

21. D
22. B
23. A
24. A
25. C

EXAMINATION SECTION
TEST 1

DIRECTIONS: Each question or incomplete statement is followed by several suggested answers or completions. Select the one that BEST answers the question or completes the statement. *PRINT THE LETTER OF THE CORRECT ANSWER IN THE SPACE AT THE RIGHT.*

1. It has been said, *Leadership, more than areas and facilities, activities, and programs – important as they are – determines the success of municipal recreation service.* The BEST justification of this statement is that

    A. children learn more skills and at a faster rate with good leadership
    B. leadership can make facilities safe
    C. leadership gives deeper significance to the play of children
    D. the program is only as good as the leadership

2. Changes or progress in our modern society have especially increased the need for recreation facilities of the type which provides

    A. development of friendships
    B. development of teamwork
    C. encouragement to creativeness
    D. individual and group competition

3. The concept of recreation MOST generally accepted today is the _____ theory.

    A. instinct-practice
    B. recapitulation of culture-epochs
    C. self-expression
    D. surplus-energy

4. The MOST serious danger of unsupervised play by children is that

    A. children learn many bad habits and acquire prejudices in their play when not supervised
    B. children playing by themselves are subject to greater hazards and potential injury
    C. misdirected play may lead to delinquency
    D. the unsupervised play environment may produce serious frustrations in children

5. There are certain generally recognized principles of recreation programming for a community.
    The FULLEST statement of these principles is:

    A. A recreation plan for the community should result in the fullest use of all resources and be integrated with long-range planning for all other community services.
    B. Education for the worthy use of leisure in homes, schools, and other community institutions is essential.
    C. Opportunities and programs for recreation should be available twelve months of the year.
    D. All of the above

6. Of the following functions, it is LEAST important for a recreation leader to
   A. develop a level of skill in children which will enable them to enjoy the activity
   B. develop winning teams
   C. maintain discipline and order
   D. provide opportunity for the greatest number to participate

7. The LEAST accurate of the following statements about the characteristics of a capable professional worker in the field of community activities is that he should have the ability to
   A. analyze thoughts and ideas in order to select basic usable concepts
   B. determine for himself, based upon his own professional experience and competence, the needs of the particular community activity
   C. express warmth of feeling in appropriate ways and without fear, as one basis for a sound relationship
   D. synthesize out of a mass of associations those which are significant and belong together in relation to a specific purpose

8. It is a GENERALLY accepted principle that volunteer leaders in a recreation program are valuable
   A. as long as they are willing to teach and direct activities without participating in them
   B. despite their need for constant supervision and guidance
   C. if they do not need constant supervision
   D. only if they possess a recreation skill

9. The MOST acceptable definition of discipline, according to the current theory of recreation, is:
   A. Methods used in special situations to achieve conformance to accepted patterns of behavior
   B. Punishment for those individuals or groups who violate legitimate rules or regulations which have been established for the general good
   C. The voluntary subordination of the individual to the welfare of the group
   D. Voluntary following of such rules as aid the development and integration of the individual

10. Motor skills are fundamental to all sports activity. It is MOST correct to say that motor skills
    A. are not generally found among pre-school children
    B. decrease in proportion to the decrease of strength and endurance with age
    C. once learned are never forgotten
    D. reach their highest state of development just after adolescence

11. From the viewpoint of professional recreation philosophy, the suggestion that two boys in disagreement should *put on the gloves* is
    A. *desirable;* it is a legitimate way of solving the disagreement
    B. *undesirable;* it assumes that the boy who wins is right in his views
    C. *undesirable;* it ignores the element of safety
    D. *undesirable;* it may involve the city in a lawsuit

12. Of the following, the BEST recreational approach to the problem of reducing juvenile delinquency is:　　　　12.____

    A. Make recreational activities more demanding and satisfying than delinquent activities
    B. Provide a well-rounded community activities program and invite potential juvenile delinquents to join
    C. Provide children with a large enough place to play and with proper equipment and they will not get into trouble
    D. There is at present no reliable solution for juvenile delinquency; all we can hope to do is keep the good boys away from the bad

13. Studies of mental health and interest in hobbies have shown that　　　　13.____

    A. interest in hobbies will keep a person mentally well
    B. the mentally well individual is less likely to have an interest in hobbies than the mentally ill person
    C. the mentally well individual is more likely to have an interest in hobbies than the mentally ill person
    D. there is no correlation between the two

14. The PRINCIPAL use to which a recreation leader should put a knowledge of common children's diseases is to　　　　14.____

    A. give occasional advice to parents on safeguarding their children's health
    B. procure a medical history of the child in order to know the activities in which the child may participate
    C. recognize symptoms of conditions which may require medical care
    D. recognize symptoms of contagious diseases which require that a child be separated from the group

15. A child falls from a tree, hitting his head on the pavement below, knocking himself unconscious.　　　　15.____
    The BEST first aid measures to take are:

    A. Apply a pressure bandage to prevent any bleeding and do not move the patient until the doctor arrives
    B. Avoid unnecessary handling and administer a mild stimulant when the child becomes conscious
    C. Do not move the patient but cover him with a coat or blanket until the doctor arrives
    D. Do not move the patient until the doctor arrives unless the patient demonstrates unusual lucidity and energy when he returns to consciousness

16. A thorough investigation should always be made of any accident occurring in a Park Department playground.　　　　16.____
    The MAIN value of such an investigation is to

    A. demonstrate to the parents the interest which the Park Department takes in the care and safety of the children
    B. discover any factors that may be corrected which contributed to the accident

C. establish the extent to which Park Department employees may be responsible for the accident
D. provide a record of the accident so that the facts may be available in the event of a lawsuit

17. The MOST important of the following principles to consider in selecting games for a group is:

   A. Games should be adapted to the age-range, the number of members, and the various factors of difference represented in the group
   B. Games should be selected which are related to the cultural and ethnic backgrounds of the participants
   C. Games should not be complicated to teach, score, or perform
   D. The previous recreational experience of the participants should form the basis of selection

18. It is a common practice for playgrounds to conduct special events or celebrations at certain times.
   The MOST important principle which should guide planners of these events is:

   A. The regular program of the playground should be suspended, if necessary, in order to provide ample opportunity for practice
   B. They should be an outgrowth of the regular playground program
   C. They require much planning; hence, they should be scheduled at least six months in advance
   D. They should seldom be financed from the playground budget, but rather an outside sponsor should be sought

19. In basketball, when playing against a zone defense, the BEST strategy is

   A. set up weak side plays by overloading one side
   B. use a fast break
   C. use more dribbling than you would against a man-to-man defense
   D. utilize screens, quick cuts, and criss-cross breaks

20. In volleyball, the MOST effective method of passing, taking into account both control and power, is by having the

   A. arm kept rigid, the ball in direct contact with the palm of the hand, and snapping the wrist in the direction of the flight
   B. the fingers in contact with the ball, swinging the arm with a lifting motion
   C. heel of the hand in firm contact with the ball, swinging the arm with a lifting motion
   D. palm of the hand in direct contact with the ball, swinging the arm with a lifting motion

21. Generally speaking, it is good technique in batting in the game of softball to

   A. select a bat that feels rather heavy
   B. swing at all balls that come within reach
   C. swing the bat so that it is parallel to the ground at the moment of impact
   D. swing with all your might at the ball

22. The one of the following which is a rule of handball doubles is:

    A. A game is 25 points
    B. A *hinder* is called if a player drives a ball into an opponent and a point is credited to the side of the man who was hit
    C. If one partner swings at the ball and misses, the other partner is permitted to return the ball
    D. To keep the ball in play, it must be struck after hitting the wall and before hitting the ground

23. The activity which is especially useful with a large, cumbersome group of untutored individuals, as a lead-up activity to the production of a play, is

    A. answer-back story   B. Blackout
    C. Little Tom Tinker   D. puppet show

24. Analysis of the motion of a schottische dance shows the following sequence of fundamental steps:

    A. High brush step to the right side, close and transfer of weight left, and a hop left
    B. Step, step, close
    C. Three small runs followed by a hop
    D. Two hops, step, close, step

25. In recommending the purchase of playground equipment, a guiding principle should be that

    A. durability is usually at least as important as suitability
    B. equipment should be bought with a view to serving the largest number of participants
    C. good equipment, carefully selected, can largely substitute for leadership
    D. small areas should be loaded with apparatus

26. In introducing a game to a group unfamiliar with it, it is LEAST important that

    A. introductory instructions be brief
    B. the game be a simple one
    C. the game be stopped while interest is still high
    D. the leader assume a confident, positive approach

27. When starting a new craft program, it is IMPORTANT that the leader

    A. employ much technical vocabulary unfamiliar to most members of the group in order to establish his expert status
    B. exclude from the group anyone whose skill in the craft is superior to the leader so as to prevent dual leadership
    C. start with material familiar to most members of the group so as to build confidence in their ability to absorb what is to come
    D. treat the group as homogeneous, disregarding individual differences

28. The one of the following which BEST expresses a desirable characteristic of group leadership is:

A. Advises the group as to suitable objectives and means of accomplishing them; assists in settling disagreements arising within the group
B. Arranges effective intercommunication among the group; does not permit any conflicts to arise
C. Permits the members of the group to set its own objectives and the means of accomplishing them; does not intercede to resolve conflicts
D. Sets proper objectives of the group and instructs in the correct method of accomplishing those objectives; settles any disputes that may arise

28.___

Questions 29-43.

DIRECTIONS: Column I lists a series of activities numbered from 29 through 43, each of which is to be matched with one of the choices given in Column II. For each item of Column I, write in the space at the right the letter in front of the choice in Column II with which it is MOST closely related.

COLUMN I

29. Bait casting
30. Block printing
31. Circle game
32. Dramatics
33. Finger painting
34. Folk song
35. Handicraft with cloth
36. Leather craft
37. Nature study
38. Net game
39. Pottery craft
40. Relay game
41. Square dance
42. Woodworking
43. Word game

COLUMN II

A. Allemande
B. Awl
C. Batik
D. Blue-tail Fly
E. Egg balancing
F. Ghost
G. Kiln
H. Linoleum
I. Loop Tennis
J. Miming
K. Miter box
L. Mumblety-peg
M. Newcomb
N. Over and Under
O. Puck
P. Skishing
Q. Soap flakes and starch
R. Terrarium
S. Three Deep
T. Titanium
U. Wicket

29.___
30.___
31.___
32.___
33.___
34.___
35.___
36.___
37.___
38.___
39.___
40.___
41.___
42.___
43.___

44. In dealing with an individual who displays his insecurity by aggressive behavior, the group leader should FIRST

   A. directly champion the individual to the group
   B. indicate acceptance of the individual by the leader
   C. insist that the individual withdraw from the group for a temporary period
   D. permit the group to attempt to deal with the individual

45. Studies of clubs and gangs have indicated certain basic facts about them.
The one of the following which is NOT a basic characteristic of clubs or gangs is:

   A. Participation in either street gangs or street clubs is a part of the growing up process of some adolescents
   B. Repressive measures in dealing with antisocial behavior of clubs or gangs brings about basic changes in attitudes and behavior
   C. Some clubs or gangs, as a result of fundamental factors such as poor housing, racial discrimination, or emotional maladjustment of their leaders or members, have developed patterns of antisocial behavior
   D. To be effective in modifying antisocial behavior of clubs or gangs, it is imperative that a social worker be assigned to only one street club or gang

46. A basketball team in a community center was composed of a group of boys who were inseparable in most of their free time. The group became involved in some antisocial activities because the most vocal and influential members of the group were able to persuade some of the other boys who individually would not have committed the wrong acts. This latter minority was PROBABLY involved because the

   A. community center had failed to break up the team so that the delinquent boys would not have had a chance to corrupt the non-delinquent
   B. community center had failed to sublimate the adolescent's need for adventure
   C. members of the group were inherently delinquentprone
   D. need to belong to the group was so great that some boys agreed to behavior which was actually unacceptable to them

47. Hostile feelings held by a few members of an organized group are LEAST likely to be reduced by

   A. appointing a committee to deal with the problem, with the disgruntled ones made members of the committee
   B. holding group discussions of the reasons for the hostility
   C. insisting upon the will of the majority
   D. making concessions to the hostile group

48. Of the following statements concerning groups, it is MOST correct to say:

   A. Hostile feelings are wrong and must be weeded out
   B. Signs of hostility prove the group was poorly chosen
   C. So long as hostile feelings are felt with equal strength by every member of a group, the group will function efficiently together
   D. The need to be together subordinates hostile feelings

49. The one of the following agencies which has initial jurisdiction over children apprehended by the Police Department is the

    A. City Youth Board
    B. Family Court
    C. Juvenile Aid Bureau
    D. Youth Bureau

50. The one of the following which BEST characterizes the philosophy of the City Youth Board is:

    A. Reform the gang; efforts to improve individuals as such have proved fruitless
    B. Search for the child in need; do not wait for the child to express a willingness to accept help
    C. Work through the children; the children will reform the parents
    D. Work through the parents; they will teach their children what is right

KEY (CORRECT ANSWERS)

1. C	11. B	21. C	31. S	41. A
2. C	12. A	22. C	32. J	42. K
3. C	13. C	23. A	33. Q	43. F
4. B	14. D	24. C	34. D	44. B
5. D	15. C	25. B	35. C	45. B
6. B	16. B	26. B	36. B	46. D
7. B	17. A	27. C	37. R	47. C
8. B	18. B	28. A	38. M	48. D
9. C	19. A	29. P	39. G	49. C
10. C	20. B	30. H	40. N	50. B

TEST 2

DIRECTIONS: Each question or incomplete statement is followed by several suggested answers or completions. Select the one that BEST answers the question or completes the statement. *PRINT THE LETTER OF THE CORRECT ANSWER IN THE SPACE AT THE RIGHT.*

1. The GREATEST value to the playground program in having an effective public relations program is that it

    A. creates public appreciation of the professional nature of recreation work
    B. encourages participation
    C. helps to interpret the program and solicit support for it
    D. is the most effective means of assuring administrative approval of a satisfactory budget

    1._____

2. In handling publicity for a recreation program, it is BEST to

    A. allow public demand to govern the rate at which information is given them
    B. coordinate all publicity with special outstanding recreational events
    C. intensify publicity efforts whenever the public loses interest
    D. maintain constant flow of information to the public at all times

    2._____

3. Of the following, the MOST important reason for the professional staff in a community center to keep detailed records of an organized group is the contribution the record makes toward

    A. better understanding of individuals and the group as a whole
    B. effective program planning for the entire center
    C. proper selection of participants for tournaments or festivals
    D. interpreting the services of the program to the public

    3._____

4. Of the following, the MOST important reason for part-time workers in a community center to keep detailed records of organized groups is the contribution the record makes toward

    A. interpreting the services of the program to the public
    B. effective program planning for the entire center
    C. proper selection of participants for tournaments or festivals
    D. providing continuity of information in the event that group leadership changes

    4._____

5. The GENERAL purposes for which staff meetings of recreation personnel should be called are share experiences and problems,

    A. reprimand the inefficient, prepare plans, and coordinate effort
    B. evaluate activities and services, explain new sports and activities, and coordinate effort
    C. evaluate activities and services, prepare plans, and coordinate effort
    D. evaluate activities and services, prepare plans, and introduce new members of the staff

    5._____

6. In planning the conduct of a staff meeting to be called for the purpose of solving a particular problem, the one of the following which should occur after all the others is the

    A. adoption of a plan of action
    B. definite allocation of responsibility
    C. discussion of the problem by the supervisor
    D. exchange of opinions

7. At a staff conference, one member of the staff frequently has good ideas but he expresses them poorly.
It would be BEST for the supervisor to

    A. disregard the manner in which the ideas are presented
    B. permit the staff member to express his ideas and for the supervisor to rephrase the ideas presented in a more readily understandable manner
    C. postpone consideration of these ideas to the next conference so that the staff member can put his ideas in clearer and better form
    D. suggest that the staff member explain his ideas to the supervisor before the staff meeting so that the supervisor may present the ideas at the meeting in a more readily understandable manner

8. The method of allowing news of forthcoming changes in policy to be spread by rumor and other unofficial means is

    A. *bad,* because it detracts from the status of the lower level supervisors
    B. *bad,* because newly appointed employees will not get the necessary information
    C. *good,* because it permits changes to be made in the policy before its official announcement in response to valid objections which may be expressed
    D. *good,* because it results in the most rapid dissemination of information about the new policy

9. Prestige is a factor which, consciously or unconsciously, is considered by most supervisors to be important.
From the point of view of good management, enhancing the prestige of a supervisor is

    A. *bad,* because it builds up the supervisor's importance without equally achieving the aims of management
    B. *good,* as a measure of economy since it may serve as a substitute for increased salary
    C. *good,* because it increases the supervisor's identification with, and support of, management aims
    D. *good,* in order to build the subordinates' awareness of, and belief in, the supervisor's authority

10. A desirable characteristic of a good supervisor is that he should

    A. identify himself with his subordinates rather than with higher management
    B. inform subordinates of forthcoming changes in policies and programs only when they directly affect the subordinates' activities
    C. make advancement of the subordinates contingent on personal loyalty to the supervisor
    D. make promises to subordinates only when sure of the ability to keep them

11. The supervisor who is MOST likely to be successful is the one who   11.____

    A. refrains from exercising the special privileges of his position
    B. maintains a formal attitude toward his subordinates
    C. maintains an informal attitude toward his subordinates
    D. represents the desires of his subordinates to his superiors

12. Application of sound principles of human relations by a supervisor may be expected to   12.____
    _____ the need for formal discipline.

    A. decrease   B. have no effect on
    C. increase   D. obviate

13. The MOST important generally approved way to maintain or develop high morale in   13.____
    one's subordinates is to

    A. give warnings and reprimands in a jocular manner
    B. excuse from staff conferences those employees who are busy
    C. keep them informed of new developments and policies of higher management
    D. refrain from criticizing their faults directly

14. In training subordinates, an important principle for the supervisor to recognize is that   14.____

    A. a particular method of instruction will be of substantially equal value for all employees in a given title
    B. it is difficult to train people over 50 years of age because they have little capacity for learning
    C. persons undergoing the same course of training will learn at different rates of speed
    D. training can seldom achieve its purpose unless individual instruction is the chief method used

15. Over an extended period of time, a subordinate is MOST likely to become and remain   15.____
    most productive if the supervisor

    A. accords praise to the subordinate whenever his work is satisfactory, withholding criticism except in the case of very inferior work
    B. avoids both praise and criticism except for outstandingly good or bad work performed by the subordinate
    C. informs the subordinate of his shortcomings, as viewed by management, while according praise only when highly deserved
    D. keeps the subordinate informed of the degree of satisfaction with which his performance of the job is viewed by management

16. A playground director has not properly carried out the orders of his assistant supervisor   16.____
    of recreation on several occasions to the point where he has been successively warned, reprimanded, and severely reprimanded. When the playground director once again does not carry out orders, the PROPER action for the assistant supervisor of recreation to take is to

    A. bring the playground director up on charges of failing to perform his duties properly
    B. have a serious discussion with the playground director explaining the need for the orders and the necessity for carrying them out

C. recommend that the playground director be transferred to another district
D. severely reprimand the playground director again, making clear that no further deviation will be countenanced

17. A supervisor with several subordinates becomes aware that two of these subordinates are neither friendly nor congenial.
In making assignments, it would be BEST for the supervisor to

   A. disregard the situation
   B. disregard the situation in making a choice of assignment but emphasize the need for teamwork
   C. investigate the situation to find out who is at fault, and give that individual the less desirable assignments until such time as he corrects his attitude
   D. place the unfriendly subordinates in positions where they have as little contact with one another as possible

18. A group of newly appointed recreation leaders have been assigned to your jurisdiction. Of the following, the MOST important thing for you to do when they report for work on their first day is to

   A. assign them to definite areas of responsibility
   B. describe to them sickness, absence, and vacation policies
   C. discuss with them the social philosophy of public recreation
   D. inform them of the general character and duties of the job

19. Assume that a new procedure in the conduct of tournaments has been adopted which you, as supervisor, think may meet with staff resistance.
To accomplish the general aims of supervision and to minimize any anticipated resistance to the new procedure, it would be BEST to

   A. approach the members of the staff individually and, on a personal basis, gain their promise of cooperation
   B. explain the reason for the new procedure at a staff meeting and advise the staff that they must accept it regardless of their personal feelings
   C. elect or appoint a staff committee to study and report on the advantages and disadvantages of the new procedure
   D. issue detailed instructions on the use of the new procedure to facilitate its application

20. When you become aware that a recreation leader under your supervision has failed to follow the proper procedure in certain cases and has concealed the fact that he has failed to do so, it would be BEST for you to

   A. discuss with him both the error and the reason for its concealment, with the aim of improving the relationship between superior and subordinate
   B. explain the proper procedure to him and reprimand him for having concealed his failure to follow it
   C. make no mention of the matter but supervise him more closely in the future
   D. tell him that the proper procedure must be followed since failure to do so is a violation of the rules of the department

21. One of the basic objectives of recreation is satisfaction or enjoyment. 21.____
    The one of the following which contributes LEAST to the accomplishment of this objective is

    A. being accepted and wanted by others of the same age
    B. complete escape through an interesting and all-consuming activity
    C. recognition from others by applause or praise
    D. receiving material recognition for effort

22. In discussing public schools and public recreation centers, recreation leaders have 22.____
    agreed that

    A. education is not an important aim of public recreation
    B. in both areas, education for the worthy use of leisure is essential
    C. motivation for learning is greater in public schools than in recreation centers
    D. the methods of teaching are the same in the two areas

23. The one of the following which the recreation leader is LEAST expected to develop in 23.____
    children participating in a playground program is

    A. acceptance of the rules of the game or activity
    B. cooperation with other children
    C. respect for the equipment being used
    D. skill in the activity

24. Using the family, rather than the individual, as the central unit in the development of a 24.____
    public recreation program is

    A. *desirable* but expensive to operate
    B. *undesirable* and expensive to operate
    C. *desirable* because it is inexpensive to operate
    D. *undesirable* except for the saving in operating expenses

25. In thinking of juvenile delinquency prevention, the MOST limited and narrow approach to 25.____
    prevention would stress

    A. improving all aspects of life that affect children's social, moral, religious, educational, and physical growth
    B. promoting healthy personality development of all children
    C. reducing recidivism should take priority over reaching children not yet law violators
    D. reaching that segment which predictive signs indicate are the potential delinquents

26. In starting a recreational program for people over sixty-five years of age, it is of FIRST 26.____
    importance to provide

    A. arts and crafts equipment and supplies
    B. a sense of belonging
    C. leadership and remove taxing responsibility
    D. very comfortable surroundings

27. In preparing a program of games, physical strength and stamina of the expected participants must be considered. When preparing a program for a group of 10-year-olds, it should be remembered that the girls of this age are

    A. as strong and active as boys of the same age
    B. more physically mature than boys of the same age
    C. passing through a period of physical weakness
    D. weaker and have less stamina than boys of the same age in all probability

28. In conducting a party for children in the eight to twelve year age group, it is LEAST important that

    A. children understand that controls on wild behavior exist
    B. instructions for games be brief and entertaining
    C. the games involve all of the children at once
    D. there be several games in which girls and boys form partnerships

29. The MOST desirable means of attracting children under ten years of age to the recreation center is to conduct a special event such as a

    A. costume parade   B. field day
    C. marbles tournament   D. song contest

30. In laying out a playground to serve a highly populated urban area, it is BEST to

    A. eliminate landscaping and arrangements that consume space
    B. make use of all available space even at the expense of not grouping activity areas by age level or degree of required supervision
    C. provide for multiple use of many play areas
    D. revise standard dimensions of sports diamonds and courts to enable the inclusion of an unusually large variety of activities

31. Of the following, the MOST important consideration in planning a playground site for children 4 to 6 years of age is

    A. confining fence or hedge
    B. grassy area
    C. hard surface area (such as asphalt)
    D. plenty of shade

32. Registration of participants as a tool for evaluating the effectiveness of a recreation program is

    A. a procedure receiving increasing acceptance for use with all activities
    B. generally too cumbersome a procedure to be of any value
    C. of value only when no attendance counts are made
    D. practical for use with many activities but impractical for use with many other activities

33. Special events are considered a desirable aspect of any playground program CHIEFLY because they

    A. add variety and a change of pace to the program
    B. are incentives to participants

C. are one of the best ways to terminate a seasonal program
D. have tremendous public relations value

34. One of the basic reasons why it is important for group leaders to focus on individual and group objectives is that doing so

   A. guarantees a better planned schedule of activities
   B. insures a fairer process in program planning
   C. reduces the likelihood that the group's individual needs will be the basis for program planning
   D. reduces the likelihood that the leader's own individual needs will be the basis on which the groups' program is determined

35. Recreation changes in character and emphasis from one age group to another.
It is MOST characteristic of the pre-school child as compared with older children that the pre-school child

   A. likes to play with others
   B. likes vigorous games
   C. plays very much by himself
   D. possesses a group spirit

36. When members of two racial groups participate in common social and recreational activities, the MOST likely effect on racial prejudice is to

   A. increase the prejudice
   B. decrease the prejudice
   C. either increase it or decrease it, depending upon the effective leadership of the groups
   D. have no effect upon the prejudice

37. Among the regular users of a community recreation center are two well-defined groups, organized on a racial basis, which have little or no contact with each other.
An attempt to dispel the existing racial prejudice may BEST be made by organizing a center-wide

   A. dance requiring cooperative action by both groups for planning and preparations
   B. party requiring cooperative action by both groups for planning and preparation
   C. dance to be sponsored and conducted by one group and to which the other group will be invited
   D. party to be sponsored and conducted by one group and to which the other group will be invited

38. The one of the following which is NOT a basic principle governing the successful operation of a teen center is:

   A. The closing time should not be too late, about 10 P.M.
   B. Separate problems should be set up for the young teenagers and for the older teenagers
   C. The center should be open whenever it will be patronized by a sizable group of teenagers
   D. The center should remain open during school holidays and vacation times

39. When a newly appointed recreation leader requests advice from an assistant supervisor of recreation on the proper way to handle several disruptive but not disturbed children who frequent the playground to which he has been assigned, the assistant supervisor of recreation should suggest that the recreation leader

    A. exclude the children from the playground since they are a disruptive influence
    B. include the children in activities and accord them special recognition
    C. make his own decisions since he knows the children best
    D. refer the children to a psychiatric clinic for help in achieving proper social adjustment

40. By a majority vote, after full discussion and participation, the members of a teenage canteen agreed upon a set of regulations. A minority threatened to withdraw from the canteen if the rules were enforced.
    The principle to be recognized in this situation is:

    A. The rules probably were too stringent and should be revised so that the minority will have its rights preserved
    B. The basic aims of democracy are not violated if we insist upon conformity once the rules have been agreed upon
    C. The basic aims of democracy are violated if we insist upon conformity once the rules have been agreed upon
    D. The basic aims of democracy require that this decision be vetoed in the interests of the minority

41. A community center program for teenagers has been criticized because the participants do not get home until several hours after the center closed.
    In such a situation, it is BEST that the center director

    A. advise the parents that he can do nothing about the time their children arrive home because he has no control over the children after they leave the center
    B. confer with the parents and with the teenagers to establish a home arrival time acceptable to community mores
    C. extend the closing time of the center to conform with the hour that the teenagers usually get home
    D. warn the teenagers that the program will be discontinued unless they go home within a short time after the closing of the center

42. It is of importance for a teen center to use a substantial part of its funds to arouse and maintain interest among a high proportion of its potential and active members.
    This objective is MOST likely to be accomplished by

    A. arranging for sweaters, pins, or other emblems with the name of the center emblazoned on it to be distributed to all members at a nominal charge
    B. careful planning to provide a wide range of activities
    C. operating on a *come and go* basis
    D. restricting the program to providing a meeting and lounging place, conducting dances, sponsoring parties, and providing opportunities for certain games

43. The organization of neighborhood recreation councils or committees should be encouraged by an assistant supervisor of recreation CHIEFLY because such councils or committees can

    A. help plan the recreation program and promote public interest in it in the neighborhood
    B. help train volunteer leaders
    C. sponsor tournaments and pageants
    D. supervise and evaluate the existing recreation programs in terms of community needs

44. The MOST valid means of evaluating the effectiveness of a program of recreation or informal education is

    A. appraisal of community support for the program as evidenced by Community Chest support (for private agencies) or tax support (for public services)
    B. appraisal of the program's purposes and performance in the light of community-wide conditions, needs, and services
    C. documented testimony of its value given by those who have participated in the program
    D. participation in the program by a substantial majority of the community

45. The author of A PHILOSOPHY OF RECREATION AND LEISURE is

    A. Bancroft   B. Butler   C. Meyer   D. Nash

46. An assistant supervisor of recreation should recognize that the training of recreation leaders is

    A. never complete, and they require continual additional training and instruction
    B. seldom complete until they have received practical on-the-job training
    C. substantially complete once they have been broken in on the job, except for the need for occasional refresher courses
    D. substantially complete at the time they are appointed since they are professional trained people

47. If a supervisor realizes that he has mistakenly blamed one of his subordinates for a certain situation, it would be BEST for the supervisor to

    A. apologize to the subordinate at the next staff meeting
    B. apologize to the subordinate at the first opportunity
    C. ignore the occurrence
    D. make no mention of the mistake but act more favorably toward the subordinate as an indication that he has realized his error

48. If a subordinate requests a transfer to a job in another division, a job of no greater apparent value to the department and no greater value to the subordinate, it would be BEST for the supervisor to

    A. recommend the transfer only if the employee can give a good reason for wanting it
    B. refer the matter to his superior without recommendation

C. refuse the transfer on the grounds that it is not in the best interest of the department
D. request the employee to explain why he wants the transfer before recommending it

49. In teaching a new job to an employee, the MOST frequent of the following sources of difficulty is the

    A. desire of the employee to do the job in his own way
    B. incompatibility of personalities of teacher and pupil
    C. lack of confidence of the employee in his ability to learn
    D. unwillingness of the employee to learn something new

50. At a staff meeting of your division, you intend to present a new plan which you have devised.
    It is MOST important for you to

    A. anticipate objections and be prepared to answer them
    B. be able to demonstrate clearly the value of the plan in your own particular area of responsibility
    C. be prepared to scrap the plan if you encounter strong opposition
    D. prepare the plan so that it will probably be accepted without alteration

KEY (CORRECT ANSWERS)

1. C	11. D	21. D	31. A	41. B
2. D	12. A	22. B	32. D	42. B
3. A	13. C	23. C	33. B	43. A
4. D	14. C	24. A	34. D	44. B
5. C	15. D	25. C	35. C	45. D
6. B	16. A	26. B	36. C	46. A
7. B	17. D	27. A	37. B	47. B
8. A	18. D	28. D	38. A	48. D
9. D	19. B	29. A	39. B	49. C
10. D	20. A	30. C	40. B	50. A

EXAMINATION SECTION
TEST 1

DIRECTIONS: Each question or incomplete statement is followed by several suggested answers or completions. Select the one that BEST answers the question or completes the statement. *PRINT THE LETTER OF THE CORRECT ANSWER IN THE SPACE AT THE RIGHT.*

1. For a large public park and recreation department, it is generally agreed that the key to productivity is

    A. contracting and leasing arrangements
    B. the effective management of personnel
    C. cost-benefit analysis
    D. appealing to private foundations for funds

    1._____

2. In a park and recreation setting, four conditions must be present in a situation in order for the department to be found legally negligent, and therefore liable, in the case of an accident. Which of the following is NOT one of these conditions?

    A. Proof of injury or damage
    B. Legal responsibility for the participant
    C. The participant's lack of an employment relationship to the department
    D. The department's failure to take reasonable care

    2._____

3. In a park and recreation department, the MOST effective approach to problem-solving is generally described as

    A. group-centered
    B. authoritarian
    C. decisions by higher authorities
    D. an analysis by planning specialists

    3._____

4. Which of the following administration philosophies or strategies is part of the future-oriented trend in park and recreation management?

    A. Planning programs with the staff, chiefly by updating past programs
    B. Evaluating outcomes primarily through attendance figures
    C. Providing programs and services based on social and economic needs of the community
    D. Requiring financial accountability and justifying budgets based on historical precedent

    4._____

5. The _____ approach to leisure service sees recreation as an important community service that is carried on both for its own sake and because it contributes to the mental and physical health of participants.

    A. human-services   B. prescriptive
    C. environmental   D. quality-of-life

    5._____

6. More or increased _____ is NOT a growing trend in leisure services.

    A. centralized personnel structure
    B. emphasis on health and fitness

    6._____

C. consideration of leisure's contribution to quality of life
D. emphasis on noncompetitive forms of play

7. The MOST common means of financing public recreation and park departments is through

   A. bonds
   B. grants
   C. taxes
   D. fees and charges

8. For evaluating the effectiveness of specific programs offered by a park and recreation department, each of the following methods is commonly used EXCEPT

   A. systems-based, goal-achievement models
   B. internal auditing by top management
   C. staff-based evaluation processes
   D. participant-based evaluation

9. A public agency that favors the delegation of authority is BEST described as

   A. heterogeneous
   B. decentralized
   C. individualistic
   D. irresponsible

10. The ability to _____ is NOT generally considered to be a core process that an entry-level employee in a park and recreation department should master.

    A. carry out both program planning and organizational planning
    B. formally articulate resource needs
    C. utilize leadership processes
    D. teach

11. A _____ budget is designed in such a way that large units of work, or special programs, are isolated, identified, and described in detail.

    A. object classification
    B. function classification
    C. program
    D. performance

12. When programming recreational activities for participants in middle childhood (6-12 years), it is important to remember that they are generally

    A. preferring separation into sexually segregated groups
    B. physically aggressive
    C. physically growing more quickly than in preschool years
    D. unconcerned about ideas such as competence, achievement, and approval from others

13. Of the following issues, _____ is LEAST likely to be negotiated in a park and recreation labor union contractual agreement.

    A. work hours
    B. contracting work, or *outsourcing*
    C. safety regulations
    D. retirement plans

14. Which of the following is considered to be the responsibility of an auxiliary staff member at a park and recreation department?

    A. Supervision of sport programs
    B. Monitoring adherence to agency rules
    C. Direction of administrative guidelines
    D. Organizing sport activities

15. Traditionally, leisure facilities have been planned according to

    A. concepts of the neighborhood and community
    B. urban planning methods based on land-use principles
    C. a needs index
    D. recommended standards of open space

16. Public agencies such as park and recreation departments typically use one of several contemporary models in evaluating whether the agency has achieved its stated objectives. Which of the following is NOT one of these models?
    Evaluation designed to measure the

    A. overall quality of programs, based on the opinion of an advisory board
    B. effectiveness of programs in meeting their stated goals and objectives
    C. effectiveness of personnel in carrying out stated program goals and objectives
    D. level of satisfaction of program participants

17. It is NOT typically a function of a public park and recreation agency's board or commission to

    A. review and approve all policies and work with the agency's managers to develop plans for meeting present and future leisure needs of the community
    B. consider and approve all personnel appointments or promotions
    C. articulate to the agency's director and staff how the details of administration should be carried out
    D. carry out long-range planning in cooperation with other community organizations to meet public recreational needs

18. In handling employment inquiries, application forms, and interviews for employment, questions to the applicant about _____ may be allowed under law, whether their use is job-related or not.

    A. employment history
    B. physical requirements
    C. arrest and conviction record
    D. age

19. According to most current practices in public agencies, any overspending or underspending in the year's budget is to be brought to the department head's attention in the month of

    A. January   B. February
    C. March or April   D. November

20. In order to avoid legal liability for certain activities involving children, some park and recreation departments use the convention of permission slips signed by a parent or guardian, in which they are asked to waive the right to sue in case of injury or accident. For several reasons, these slips offer the department a false sense of security. Which of the following is NOT one of these reasons?

    I. In all cases, signed statements are invalid if the risks of the activity are not understood.
    II. The waiver is not valid unless signed by both parents, no matter what their geographic location.
    III. They cannot waive the right of a child to bring suit against the agency when the child reaches the legal age for doing so.

    The CORRECT answer is:

    A. I only   B. I, II   C. I, III   D. I, II, III

21. Which of the following recreation facilities would most likely be located at or near the intersection of major or secondary thoroughfares near the center of a 4- or 5-square mile service area?

    A. Playlot
    B. Large park
    C. Playground
    D. Athletic field

22. Which of the following is NOT a level of planning commonly associated with recreation and park facilities?

    A. Planning that focuses solely on recreation and park development within a total community, sometimes as a separate portion of a total plan
    B. Regional planning that takes into account services and facilities offered by adjacent jurisdictions
    C. Planning that is concerned with the development of a particular facility or the needs of a single neighborhood
    D. Total master planning that considers all aspects of municipal growth, including industrial and residential development, transportation, education, housing, health, etc.

23. The MAIN advantage of a structured, centralized approach to recreational programming is

    A. being able to respond to local neighborhood needs
    B. optimum legal protection from liability claims
    C. more efficient use of personnel resources
    D. a set of clear-cut standards for fulfilling the agency's stated objectives

24. When programming recreational activities for participants in middle adulthood (40-65 years), it is important to remember that they generally

    A. experience physiological changes in the brain
    B. begin to experience instability in cognitive skills
    C. display a loss of creativity
    D. tend to gain weight easily

25. In park and recreation accounting, concurrent auditing represents 25.____
    A. a preaudit of expected income or disbursements
    B. a formal check of specific administrative or program divisions of a department, or construction or maintenance projects
    C. a form of bookkeeping report showing the assets and liabilities of a given fund or budget
    D. all departmental expenditures that have been authorized and carried out

KEY (CORRECT ANSWERS)

1. B
2. C
3. A
4. C
5. D

6. A
7. C
8. B
9. B
10. B

11. C
12. A
13. B
14. A
15. C

16. A
17. C
18. A
19. B
20. C

21. D
22. B
23. D
24. D
25. A

TEST 2

DIRECTIONS: Each question or incomplete statement is followed by several suggested answers or completions. Select the one that BEST answers the question or completes the statement. *PRINT THE LETTER OF THE CORRECT ANSWER IN THE SPACE AT THE RIGHT.*

1. Each of the following is a benefit associated with the use of a *matrix* structure in a public park and recreation department EXCEPT

    A. greater opportunity of employees' personal development
    B. better technical performance
    C. improved flexibility in conditions of change and uncertainty
    D. involvement in long-range planning of employees at every level

    1._____

2. Which of the following statements about recreationists in early adulthood (20-39 years) is generally TRUE?

    A. They are more self-centered than adolescents.
    B. Their friendships are characterized by less intimacy.
    C. They experience a lack of stability in intellectual skills.
    D. They expand their social relationships through new contacts within the occupational and community settings.

    2._____

3. When programming recreation activities, an administrator's choices are likely to be affected by each of the following factors EXCEPT

    A. the number of potential activities
    B. the characteristics of participants
    C. the funds required
    D. personnel

    3._____

4. A recreation programmer wants to stage a single-elimination summer softball tournament at the department's facilities. Each of the following is an advantage associated with the single-elimination format EXCEPT it

    A. is usually more interesting for spectators
    B. may accommodate a large number of participants
    C. encourages maximum participation
    D. is the most economical to conduct

    4._____

5. In a recreation or park facility's off-season, an administrator wants to maintain a minimum level of care. Typically, how often should litter at the facility be picked up?

    A. Daily
    B. Weekly
    C. Monthly
    D. Every two months

    5._____

6. Funding agencies for public park and recreation departments have historically applied strict criteria for determining grant recipients. Which of the following statements about their considerations is generally FALSE?

    A. There must be evidence that existing programs and facilities are being fully utilized.
    B. Agencies applying for grants must be prepared to guarantee a substantial portion of the total grant proposal.

    6._____

C. Higher priority is given to proposals that come from more than one agency or sponsor.
D. Wherever possible, grant proposals should be designed to serve the general population, rather than isolated or special-need communities.

7. In public recreation programs, sport accounts for about _____% of all active involvement.

   A. 10-30   B. 35-50   C. 60-75   D. 80-95

8. Which of the following is NOT a level of responsibility defined by the functional classification of personnel analysis?

   A. Managerial   B. Tutorial
   C. Logistical   D. Operational

9. During a community needs assessment, a park and recreation department would most likely conduct use surveys among the community members in order to determine the _____ leisure needs of the community.

   A. expressed   B. normative   C. relative   D. perceived

10. The main disadvantage to using an *object classification* type of budget for a park and recreation department is that

    A. it does not relate expenditures meaningfully to programs
    B. certain expenditures, such as personnel, are not considered *objects*
    C. it does not provide complete itemization of expenditures
    D. it does not take unplanned expenditures into account

11. Which of the following is NOT a guideline to follow in preparing a newspaper release for a public park and recreation department event or service?

    A. The release should stick to the facts and avoid editorializing.
    B. An attempt should be made to feature a prominent or interesting individual or group of people in the article.
    C. The most important information should be included at the beginning of the article.
    D. The release should be limited to 2 or 3 pages.

12. In a public school or college's recreational facilities, the priority of use must be

    A. intramural or campus recreational programming
    B. intercollegiate practice sessions or competition
    C. formal academic program use
    D. community residents

13. For a supervisor in a park and recreation department, each of the following is a guideline to follow in taking disciplinary action with employees EXCEPT

    A. when correction is required, it should be handled in private
    B. the worker should be told what he or she can do to correct the situation
    C. the action should not be taken until some time after the need for it has been established
    D. take the same corrective actions for the same behaviors with different individuals

14. The healthiest way a park and recreation department manager can approach the subject of inter-employee conflict is to view it as   14.____

    A. inevitable, but desirable and able to be used to constructive ends
    B. a healthy sign that workers in the department intend to challenge and compete with one another to meet departmental goals
    C. an inevitable product of a close working relationship that should be not denied, but endured peaceably
    D. a harmful and destructive influence that should be avoided at all costs

15. Which of the following is NOT generally considered to be a guideline to follow in determining when, and for what, recreation fees and charges are justified?   15.____

    A. Frequently charge where *preservation* is the dominant function
    B. Be sure that some benefit accrues to the taxpayer
    C. The specific services to be charged for and the fee should be matters of local choice
    D. Frequently charge where *use* is the dominant function

16. Generally, which of the following approaches to urban planning is used LEAST often?   16.____

    A. Developing an ideal model of the community
    B. Cost-revenue model
    C. User-oriented approach
    D. Needs index model

17. When conditions within a working group are only moderately favorable or unfavorable (i.e., the leader is well-liked but the task under consideration is unstructured), what type of leadership style is most appropriate?   17.____

    A. Laissez-faire   B. Task-oriented
    C. Authoritarian   D. Relationship-oriented

18. In a park and recreation department, a cost-benefit analysis is LEAST likely to be useful for   18.____

    A. identifying high- and low-cost programs and services as related to maintenance, administration, and direct leadership costs per participant-hour of service rendered
    B. providing valuable support data for justifying budget requests
    C. providing essential data for determining the cost-effectiveness of individual department personnel
    D. permitting the assignment of priorities to specific programs and services

19. In recent years, the number of volunteers working for public park and recreation departments has increased among certain segments of the population. Among the following groups, which has shown the LEAST significant increase in volunteer service?   19.____

    A. Females   B. Males
    C. Poor people   D. Minorities

20. The major type of legislation affecting parks and recreation is the   20.____

    A. regulatory law   B. special district law
    C. enabling law   D. home rule legislation

21. When programming recreational activities for participants in late adulthood (over 65 years), it is important to remember that they generally

    A. do not require a significant restructuring of time
    B. have a self-concept that tends to be more dependent upon external factors
    C. prefer to live in close contact with others of their age group
    D. become less active if they are men, and more active if they are women

22. The self-study approach to agency evaluation, outlined by the National Recreation and Park Association, includes standards that are used in measuring the effectiveness of a department in several major categories. Which of the following is NOT one of these categories?

    A. Administration   B. Evaluation
    C. Programming   D. Funding

23. Decisions made at the lower level of an agency's management, which are part of operational planning and program implementation, are described as _____ decisions.

    A. primary   B. problem-oriented
    C. reflex   D. task-oriented

24. In park and recreation applications, a *flowchart* is used to

    A. view the community-wide availability of programs and detect under- or over-provision of different types of activities on a geographical basis
    B. show all events or continuing activities in a convenient and easily understood form
    C. show individual projects or programs laid out along a calendar, with specific tasks indicated for the dates on which they are to be begun and completed
    D. identify major facilities and ongoing programs

25. In recreation and sports injury cases involving parents and children, the parents, but not the child, can be barred from recovery for a child's injury under certain conditions. Which of the following is NOT one of these conditions?
    The

    A. parent has failed to exercise reasonable care to prevent the child from placing himself in a situation in which lack of self-protective capacity may reasonably be expected to result in harm to the child
    B. child is too young to exercise self-protection
    C. child's incapacity is a contributing factor in harm
    D. injury involves an *attractive nuisance*

KEY (CORRECT ANSWERS)

1. D
2. D
3. A
4. C
5. A

6. D
7. C
8. B
9. D
10. A

11. D
12. C
13. C
14. A
15. A

16. B
17. D
18. C
19. A
20. C

21. D
22. D
23. D
24. C
25. D

EXAMINATION SECTION
TEST 1

DIRECTIONS: Each question or incomplete statement is followed by several suggested answers or completions. Select the one that BEST answers the question or completes the statement. *PRINT THE LETTER OF THE CORRECT ANSWER IN THE SPACE AT THE RIGHT.*

1. A *typical* definition of recreation agreed upon by MOST authorities would be
    A. voluntarily chosen leisure activities, for pleasure or personal benefit, meeting community standards and needs
    B. pleasurable activities provided by community agencies without social purpose
    C. whatever people want to do, because they want to do it
    D. purposeful activities, such as anti-delinquency, addiction treatment, or golden age programs, which make use of trips and cultural activities

1.____

2. In the past, it was argued that recreation programs for youth prevented juvenile delinquency.
Today the majority of social work or recreation authorities would MOST probably support the view that
    A. recreation is the key element in any anti-delinquency program
    B. recreation has proved to be of little value in anti-delinquency programs
    C. juvenile delinquents usually are anti-social and disruptive and should be kept out of organized recreation programs
    D. juvenile delinquency treatment requires varied services, including education, job training, recreation, and improved housing

2.____

3. The MAJOR professional organization serving the recreation field in the United States today is the
    A. American Institute of Park and Recreation Practitioners
    B. National Recreation and Park Association
    C. National Recreation Association
    D. American Association for Health, Physical Education, and Recreation

3.____

4. Varied theories of play have been developed by psychologists, philosophers, and others.
One TRADITIONAL theory that sees play as the means through which children prepare for the demands of adult life is the _____ theory.
    A. instinct-practice   B. catharsis
    C. recapitulation   D. relaxation

4.____

5. Which of the following statements BEST supports the self-expression theory of play as developed by Mason and Mitchell?
    A. Activities are engaged in for the purpose of overcoming natural human inertness.

5.____

49

B. Due to the pressures for self-maintenance and other compulsions, human beings use play as outlets for frustration.
C. Human physiological and anatomical structure are independent of any specific form of play.
D. Because human beings are dynamic animals, activity is a primary need of life.

6. Of the following, the MOST recent psychological theory of play is the   6.____
   A. pleasure principle theory (Freud)
   B. play extraversion theory (Piaget)
   C. arousal or stimulation theory (Berlynne)
   D. aggressive-release theory (Schiller-Spencer-Groos)

7. Generally, the BASIC philosophy of public recreation departments today is to   7.____
   A. serve all groups as fully as possible
   B. place the greatest emphasis on helping the poor
   C. serve primarily the middle and upper classes
   D. concentrate on children and youth

8. The one of the following which is NOT a widely accepted goal of public recreation departments is to   8.____
   A. provide constructive and creative outlets for leisure
   B. meet participants' physical, mental, social, and creative needs
   C. develop large numbers of athletes to play on college or pro teams
   D. strengthen family life and help community unity

9. The growth of the organized recreation movement in the United States was promoted by several social factors.   9.____
   Of the following, the one which did NOT contribute to such growth is
   A. the increase in leisure through the shortened work-week, more holidays, and longer vacations
   B. the development of movies, television, and radio as major forms of entertainment
   C. the general affluence and mobility in society
   D. more liberal attitudes toward leisure on the part of religious, educational, and government authorities

10. Recognition by state certifying boards or departments is one of the formal methods through which professionals in fields such as law or medicine are approved.   10.____
    Today, certification for recreation professionals exists in
    A. a small number of states   B. all fifty states
    C. no states   D. about half the states

11. Supervisors should be able to advise recently appointed recreation workers on the appropriate selection of activities for specific age groups.   11.____
    When planning for after-school recreation activities for boys of elementary-school age, the MOST useful type of game would usually be

    A. low-organized games, such as dodge-ball, kick-ball, and relays
    B. table games, such as parcheessi, backgammon, and chess
    C. encounter games and touching games, like those used in sensitivity groups
    D. mental games and contests, such as ghost, coffee-pot, and twenty questions

12. Since anti-social youth are often unwilling to enter highly structured activities and programs, or may be barred from recreation centers, they are frequently not served by community recreation agencies.
    Of the following, the BEST way to serve such youth is to
    A. develop entirely new kinds of activities that will appeal to delinquents because of their thrill-seeking nature
    B. organize special community center programs to serve only delinquent youth who have been in trouble with the law
    C. assign roving or street gang workers to make contact with unaffiliated youth and gangs to involve them in constructive activities
    D. wait until they are sent to correctional institutions and then give them concentrated recreation programs there

12.____

13. Adolescent girls in youth houses (detention or remand centers) often have poor self-concepts.
    Of the following, the TYPICAL approach used by recreation workers in such settings to help these girls improve their self-concepts is to
    A. tell such girls at appropriate times that they are just as good as anybody
    B. organize self-improvement classes to teach skills in make-up, dressing, or modeling
    C. sponsor sports teams, such as basketball or volleyball, which can compete with other institutions
    D. administer personality tests to diagnose their problems

13.____

14. Many teenage boys are fascinated by automobiles.
    Of the following, a USEFUL way for a creation worker to deal with this interest would be to
    A. sponsor drag-racing meets in a conveniently located park or raceway
    B. develop an automotive hobby car repair club in a community center or nearby garage
    C. arrange a contest to select one boy to go on a trip to the Indianapolis 500 to watch the big race
    D. develop a joint program with a school bus company to train boys as junior bus operators

14.____

15. According to the traditional *space standards* employed for the past several decades to measure the need for open space and recreation facilities in American communities, there should be AT LEAST
    A. one neighborhood playground for each 1,500 children under age 12
    B. three acres of outdoor recreation space for each 1,000 residents
    C. one acre of outdoor recreation space for each 100 residents
    D. one community center for each 5,000 children and teenagers

15.____

16. *Therapeutic recreation service* is the term applied today to programs which serve the physically, mentally, or socially handicapped.
    For BEST results, such programs should be provided in
    A. institutions such as mental hospitals or schools for the mentally handicapped
    B. community settings such as after-care centers or community programs for the physically disabled
    C. both institutional and community settings
    D. private or voluntary facilities

16.____

17. Social group work is BEST defined as a method of social work which
    A. assigns people to groups for intensive psychotherapy as a means of crisis intervention
    B. helps people improve their social functioning and ability to cope with inter-personal problems
    C. utilizes unskilled community people to take over many social work organizations
    D. relies on the leader's ability to mobilize people into effective instruments for community reform

17.____

18. Some recreation departments operate multi-service senior centers which provide social services related to nutrition, health needs, legal, or housing assistance, as well as recreation.
    This type of program is regarded by leading authorities in the field of recreation as
    A. usually not the function of a recreation department since it has proved to be a hindrance to customary social and recreational programs
    B. clearly not the function of a recreation department and should be discontinued
    C. an appropriate function of a recreation department and is justified by Federal funding guidelines in this field
    D. an appropriate function of a recreation department only when the program is receiving a grant from the State Department of Aging

18.____

19. The view that MOST social workers generally have of recreation is that it is
    A. almost identical to social work
    B. a competitor with social work for public funds
    C. a medium through which they can involve and work constructively with participants
    D. strictly for fun, without a serious purpose

19.____

20. The three MAJOR areas of social work training and practice are
    A. group work, psychiatric case work, and neighborhood management
    B. community analysis, case work, and agency supervision
    C. group rehabilitation, psychiatric community development, and case work
    D. case work, group work, and community organization

20.____

5 (#1)

21. Which of the following BEST expresses the program objectives of recreation programs provided by the municipal agencies as a whole?
They should
    A. emphasize after-school and summer vacation play programs
    B. provide activities for various age groups
    C. concentrate on programs for younger boys and teenage youth
    D. meet social needs that are unsatisfied by family relationships

21.____

22. Of the following, which is the LEAST appropriate basis for choosing the recreation program activities for a community center, hospital, or other institutions? The
    A. needs and interests of the participants based on their age, sex, socio-economic background, etc.
    B. overall philosophy and goals of the sponsoring agency
    C. ability of the agency to offer certain activities based on its staff resources, facilities, funding, etc.
    D. degree to which prospective participants are personally acquainted with one another

22.____

23. The MOST common approach to developing schedules of program activities in municipal recreation departments is to organize them
    A. on a centralized basis, that is, each central office or county headquarters develops a precise schedule that must be followed in each center or playground
    B. on a *report* system, that is, each center or playground develops its individual schedule and must report daily on which activities were carried out, and which were not
    C. on the basis of seasonal interests, with different schedules being developed for summer, fall, winter, and spring
    D. according to whatever seems to be of interest on a particular day, emphasizing flexibility

23.____

24. A difficult problem in scheduling recreation programs is to have personnel available at needed times.
The BEST approach for dealing with this problem is to
    A. change recreation leadership jobs to the four-day workweek that has become so popular in industry
    B. make leadership assignment schedules more flexible to insure coverage for special events, including evening and weekend activities
    C. assign all personnel a noon-to-8 P.M. daily schedule
    D. convert all full-time leadership jobs into part-time per session positions and then assign these as needed

24.____

25. Ideally, the BEST program schedule for a community recreation center would be one which covers
    A. the full day and evening to permit scheduling for senior citizens, housewives, or pre-schoolers, as well as youth and other adults
    B. from 3:00 P.M. to 10:00 P.M. since this is the time when children and youth are out of school

25.____

53

C. the daily hours of maximum use, based on participant demand, because of the financial limitations of many centers
D. daytime hours only since most people today will not come out at night because of fear of crime

KEY (CORRECT ANSWERS)

1.	A	11.	A
2.	D	12.	C
3.	B	13.	B
4.	A	14.	B
5.	D	15.	C
6.	C	16.	C
7.	A	17.	B
8.	C	18.	C
9.	B	19.	C
10.	A	20.	D

21. B
22. D
23. C
24. B
25. A

TEST 2

DIRECTIONS: Each question or incomplete statement is followed by several suggested answers or completions. Select the one that BEST answers the question or completes the statement. *PRINT THE LETTER OF THE CORRECT ANSWER IN THE SPACE AT THE RIGHT.*

1. Active team games during the summer months of July and August at a neighborhood playground are BEST scheduled for
    A. early afternoon and late evening
    B. Saturday only (morning and afternoon)
    C. morning, late afternoon, and evening
    D. evening only (after 7:30 P.M.

    1.____

2. Various activities help to keep attendance at a summer playground high by building interest and enthusiasm among participants.
   Which of the following is the POOREST example of such activities?
    A. Weekly special events, such as pet shows, bicycle rodeos, hobby fairs, etc.
    B. End-of-summer festivals, carnivals, play-days, exhibitions, etc., for which participants prepare for several weeks
    C. Trips using chartered or public transportation to state parks, swimming pools, etc. for those attending regularly
    D. Daily tutoring programs of remedial education for those who are having difficulty in school

    2.____

3. Of the various types of activities sponsored by public recreation departments, the MOST popular single category, according to national surveys, is
    A. services for the handicapped (such as the mentally handicapped, blind, or physical disabled)
    B. the performing arts (music, drama, and dance)
    C. social activities (clubs, parties, dances, etc.)
    D. sports of all kinds (such as baseball, football, and basketball)

    3.____

4. The MOST typical method of organizing youth sports leagues in public recreation departments is to
    A. encourage recreation leaders to organize and coach several teams themselves, running their own tournaments
    B. reduce competitive play, which is harmful to youth, and concentrate instead on cooperative games
    C. work with community organizations that set up and coach their own teams
    D. have children on each block form their own teams and do their own coaching

    4.____

5. Each craft activity has a specific set of items describing its equipment or process. The following words, *bisque*, *greenware*, and *slab-construction*, are used in reference to
    A. ceramics   B. metalcrafts
    C. glass-blowing   D. decoupage

    5.____

6. According to their degree of difficulty, various arts and crafts activities are usually suited to different age levels,
   Which of the following would be MOST suited to pre-school children?
   A. Macrame
   B. Watercolor painting
   C. Fingerpainting
   D Jewelry-making

6.____

7. Among the most popular recreational sport activities are basketball, baseball, and bowling.
   The terms which do NOT apply to any of these three games are
   A. strike, dribble, sacrifice
   B. linebacker, offside, foot-fault
   C. spare, infield, hoop
   D. walking, infield, alley

7.____

8. Which of the following activities would LEAST likely be found in a municipal recreation department's music program?
   A. Rock-and-roll band practice and competition
   B. Chamber music groups
   C. Drum and bugle corps
   D. Informal community singing or folk music activities

8.____

9. Informal dramatics activities are often used with children and teenagers.
   Which of the following would be MOST likely to promote creative dramatic skills and interest among beginners?
   A. One-act play contests with scripts, costumes, and scenery
   B. Choral reading of popular poetry
   C. Memorizing and reciting sections from famous Broadway plays
   D. Improvisational dramatic games, like prop or paper bag plays

9.____

10. In the past, many recreation departments sponsored holiday festivals or special events such as the English May Day Festival.
    Today, the trend is to
    A. have such festivals reflect ethnic group interests such as Black Culture or Hispanic-American Arts
    B. eliminate all such events since there is little interest in them
    C. deal mainly with historical commemorations since these would appeal to traditional patriotism
    D. make festivals *future-minded* by dealing with the Space Age or America of the Future

10.____

11. Of the following types of tournaments, the type which can be completed MOST quickly in individual sports such as fencing or table-tennis is the _____ tournament.
    A. round robin
    B. elimination
    C. challenge (pyramid)
    D. challenge (ladder)

11.____

12. Recreation has been affected by several key trends in psychiatric treatment.
    Which of the following is NOT such a key trend?
    A. Reducing patient populations in large, distant state institutions and setting up local mental health facilities, with after-care or day-clinic programs

12.____

B. Reliance on chemotherapy, which makes patients more receptive to programs
   C. The development of activity therapy programs in many hospitals, which include education, recreation, occupational therapy, and similar activities
   D. Hiring of psychiatric patients as recreation aides, which may lead to employment after discharge

13. In recreation programs serving the seriously physically handicapped, such as those who have suffered strokes, amputations, etc., the PRIMARY program objective is to
    A. help patients develop potential skills using the facilities of community and out-of-hospital recreational programs
    B. raise funds, through parties, bazaars, special shows, etc., that patients put on to meet special patient needs
    C. use recreation as a specific treatment modality that will restore function, help patients learn to use prosthesis, etc.
    D. make patients accept their limitations and the fact that they cannot participate in many normal recreation activities

14. The majority of mentally handicapped teenagers or young adults live in the community, rather than in institutions. Recreation for such persons has several important goals.
    Of the following, the LEAST appropriate recreation goal for such persons is to
    A. help them improve the poor coordination and overcome the obesity typical of many such persons through physical activity
    B. help them acquire social skills and improve behavior and appearance so they will be able to mingle with others more effectively
    C. provide enjoyable and socially desirable leisure activities in order to make life more satisfying
    D. improve their I.Q.'s in order to help them get better jobs or be able to continue in school

15. Senior centers that serve older persons should meet the important needs of these individuals.
    Of the following, it would be LEAST appropriate for such centers to meet the need for
    A. full-time employment by acting as a placement bureau for center members
    B. modified physical activity to help keep older people active and prevent physical deterioration
    C. social activity to help aging people make friends and avoid isolation
    D. program activities in which older people may do volunteer service in hospitals or in the community

16. In planning a recreation program at a low-income public housing project, it is important to establish an advisory board or council.
Such board or council should represent PRIMARILY the needs and interests of the
   A. civic groups
   B. residents
   C. parent-teacher associations
   D. youth workers

17. Public relations may have many objectives for a public recreation department. Of the following, the LEAST appropriate objective would be to
   A. provide accurate information about the department's overall program to the public at large
   B. encourage attendance and involvement at the department's events and regular programs
   C. build favorable public attitudes and encourage volunteer leadership in the programs
   D. encourage petitions or letter-writing campaigns for increased budgets for the department

18. The one of the following which is the MOST effective method for producing successful public relations is for recreation program administrators to
   A. appear before civil organizations
   B. satisfy users of programs
   C. publish effective brochures, announcements, and reports
   D. employ qualified, indigenous para-professionals

19. If a recreation supervisor were going to publicize a large one-day recreation event in his borough, the BEST way to promote attendance would be to
   A. use newspaper releases and distribute fliers to schools, churches, and temples
   B. place posters advertising the event in store windows
   C. put posters on playground bulletin boards
   D. make a filmstrip about the forthcoming event and distribute prints to civic groups

20. Assume that, as a recreation supervisor, you are directing a community center that has poor participation in programs by local residents.
Of the following, the MOST effective way for you to arouse more public interest would be to
   A. have the publicity office in your department's central office send out newspaper releases about the center
   B. form a neighborhood council to interpret the community's needs to you and help publicize your program
   C. frequent places where local people congregate
   D. plan a panel discussion in a nearby community auditorium to discuss the problem

21. There are several possible approaches to getting community involvement in recreation service.
Of the following, the approach that would usually be LEAST workable would be to
    A. draw up a list of interested parents, clergymen, businessmen, local educators, etc., and invite them to a planning meeting about the neighborhood's recreation program
    B. announce an election to a recreation council, and select a slate of nominees, one for each square block so that local residents can elect their own representatives
    C. inquire as to whether the local Parent-Teachers Association will form a subcommittee interested in youth recreation to assist you
    D. work closely with the local district planning board to insure that they consider recreation as an important community service and to get their advice and help

22. Whether patients will be able to use their leisure constructively after discharge from the hospital is of vital concern to recreation workers in psychiatric hospitals.
Which of the following approaches would be LEAST useful in assuring continuing recreation service to a patient?
    A. Get a mimeographed list of recreation agencies in a patient's neighborhood and give him this before he is discharged
    B. Visit and talk with staff members of recreation agencies in a patient's neighborhood to make plans for their receiving the discharged patient
    C. Develop joint hospital-community recreation programs in special events, tours, entertainment programs, etc. to build a base of understanding for discharged patients
    D. Help the patient develop skills and interests in activities that will actually be available in his neighborhood after discharge

23. Therapeutic recreation seeks to help disabled persons enjoy a fuller, happier life. The question of whether they should be segregated in separate programs for the handicapped is an important one.
Which of the following statements about this group is MOST valid?
    A. The non-handicapped in society are usually very sympathetic to the disabled and welcome them in all recreational and social programs.
    B. The handicapped are better off by themselves, in groups with others having similar disabilities, so they will not feel inferior.
    C. It is an important goal to integrate the handicapped with other persons whenever possible, although sometimes it may not be feasible.
    D. The handicapped should, without exception, be mixed with the non-handicapped in recreation programs.

24. Recreation is usually considered to be a positive force for improving social relations between different racial, ethnic, or socio-economic groups.
Of the following, which is the MOST valid statement about recreation and inter-group relations?

A. Public recreation is one field in which racial discrimination is not prohibited by law.
B. Recreation workers have an obligation to reflect and agree with the views of those they serve, regardless of the nature of such views.
C. Many of our community recreation programs are heavily racially segregated.
D. Prejudice is an inborn trait which often appears in competitive sports.

25. For minority-group youth, sports often provide upward social mobility into college and subsequent business careers.
However, of the following, a MAJOR problem that arises for such youth in their seeking upward social mobility is that
   A. unscrupulous college sports programs often exploit them
   B. they are unable to satisfactorily relate to members of their peer group
   C. sports fail to provide an outlet for hostility and aggression
   D. religious cults to which they become converted distract them from sports

KEY (CORRECT ANSWERS)

1.	C		11.	B
2.	D		12.	D
3.	D		13.	A
4.	C		14.	D
5.	A		15.	A
6.	C		16.	B
7.	B		17.	D
8.	B		18.	B
9.	D		19.	A
10.	A		20.	B

21. B
22. A
23. C
24. C
25. A

TEST 3

DIRECTIONS: Each question or incomplete statement is followed by several suggested answers or completions. Select the one that BEST answers the question or completes the statement. *PRINT THE LETTER OF THE CORRECT ANSWER IN THE SPACE AT THE RIGHT.*

1. The trend in many recreation and park departments during the past several years has been toward providing special facilities and programs based on user fees and charges.
   The criticism MOST often made against such fees and charges is that
   A. few recreation directors have made serious efforts to serve residents of disadvantaged neighborhoods
   B. it increases the cost of servicing and maintaining facilities and services because standards must be raised
   C. public employees may be tempted to misappropriate funds or may be subject to accusations of dishonesty
   D. poor people may be unable to participate in what should be a publicly-available service

   1.____

2. With few exceptions, recreation directors have not been able to gain permission to operate programs regularly in school buildings.
   Of the following, the MOST successful way to improve this situation is to
   A. develop relationships and cooperative programs with local school board and district officials, or with individual school principals and custodians
   B. bring a class-action suit against the local schoolboard
   C. collect and submit legally valid petitions to the administration
   D. exert pressure on the schools by denying them use of parks or other recreational facilities for their physical education activities

   2.____

3. Many hospitals, particularly psychiatric hospitals, have therapists keep regular reports of patient participation in recreation programs.
   Of the following, the BEST use of such reports is to
   A. provide information which may be presented at meetings of the treatment team when the progress of patients is discussed
   B. provide a basis for a daily discussion between the patient and the therapist so the patient knows what is expected of him
   C. justify adverse actions such as denial of recreation privileges or the imposition of personal restrictions
   D. meet the requirements of mental hygiene laws as to standards of treatment and patient progress

   3.____

4. Much correspondence is likely to come into the central office of a public recreation department.
   Generally, all letters should be answered within one or two days UNLESS
   A. a letter is of a commonplace and unimportant nature
   B. the writer is unreasonably critical of the department
   C. form letters are used in place of personalized correspondence
   D. a letter requires special inquiries or decision-making

   4.____

5. One major type of report in recreation programs is based on the attendance of participants.
Such report are GENERALLY considered to be
   A. an excellent quantitative and qualitative basis for evaluating the success of a program
   B. of primary use in operational research involving participant behavior and outcomes
   C. unnecessary since few departments continue to use attendance reports as a basis for funding
   D. quite inaccurate unless attendance counts are done systematically and staff members avoid inflating them

5.____

6. An informal survey of recreation in a hospital showed that patients who engaged regularly in the program were discharged from the hospital earlier than those who did not.
Based on this information only, it would be MOST valid to say that
   A. such information has validity or meaning only to a qualified medical research person
   B. it is inconclusive whether there exists a cause and effect relationship between participation and discharge
   C. probably the healthier patients took part in the recreation program, and this was the reason for their earlier discharge
   D. recreation was the major determinant of earlier discharge

6.____

7. The one of the following it would be BEST to do when preparing or developing an annual report of a large recreational program is to
   A. gather material such as photos, program descriptions, news stories, and statistics which appeared during the courses of the year
   B. use narrative description rather than charts or graphs to present statistical data
   C. present only the positive aspects and successes of your program, elaborating when necessary to give a favorable picture
   D. give praise to key political figures in the report so they will support the program in the future

7.____

8. *Crash* programs of recreation have sometimes been rushed into slum areas as a response to the threat of violence. Often, the approach has been to present *portable* programs, for example, portable pools put into lots of streets, mobile libraries and nature displays, puppet shows, movies, and rock or soul music shows.
Of the following, the MAJOR weakness of the *portable* recreation approach is that
   A. funds expended for such programs tend to be excessive and the general public is antagonized
   B. it emphasizes expending aimless energy rather than promoting social growth
   C. it meets only temporary recreation needs and fails to effect a permanent resolution of recreation problems

8.____

D. it tends to draw large numbers of youth out on the street, where they become riotous

9. A recent change in the concept of recreation as a public service is that it is now being thought of as a kind of social therapy.
The MOST recent illustration of this has been the
   A. joint effort of religious agencies to develop new recreation programs, including year-round camping, for broken families
   B. expanded recreation programs in youth houses, remand institutions, and similar institutions run by the Department of Social Services
   C. new recreation program in private or multi-room occupancy hotels
   D. crash effort to provide recreation programs for alcoholics and older drug addicts

9._____

10. Low-income and racial minority youth tend to have very limited recreation interests. Often, teenage boys want to take part in basketball, but little else of an organized nature.
For a recreation center director, what would be the BEST professional approach to this attitude?
   A. Begin with the interests they already have, then try to broaden their involvement in other recreation, athletic, or cultural activities
   B. Stick to basketball, their true interest, since they resist other activities
   C. Since they are able to play basketball in many neighborhood settings, eliminate this part of the program and offer new kinds of sports, cultural activities, and social events
   D. Rely on carefully prepared interest survey, and then offer youth only the activities and events they say they want

10._____

11. A NEW trend in many cities, with respect to the assignment of recreation leadership personnel, is to
   A. assign workers to one setting on a full-time, year-round basis so that they will be completely familiar with the work and do a superior job
   B. use seniority more than ever before, thereby giving the long-time employee freedom to pick his job
   C. rotate the assignments of workers from season-to-season or even day-to-day maximize output and improve morale by giving challenging assignments
   D. create new job shifts, such as one week from 9:00 to 5:00, next week from 2:00 to 10:00, etc.

11._____

12. Recreation counseling is becoming more widely used in many hospitals. Such counseling is PRIMARILY intended to
   A. help patients explore their leisure attitudes and interests and motivate them toward fuller participation after discharge
   B. teach patients a broad range of activities, such as sports, crafts, and social skills, that they can use after discharge
   C. use the recreation situation to uncover problems that can then be discussed when the patient gets therapeutic counseling

12._____

D. allow the patients to advise staff members on how best to organize the recreation program

13. A major problem today in many recreation and park departments is costly and destructive vandalism.
Which of the following methods of dealing with this problem has NOT been widely accepted throughout the United States?
    A. Provide stronger enforcement of rules and better surveillance and protection of recreation and park facilities
    B. Offer more attractive programs since people are less likely to vandalize a facility if it is staffed and providing popular community activities
    C. Use new types of designs so that facilities are less prone to vandalism, such as windowless buildings, concrete benches and tables, etc.
    D. Abandon parks or playgrounds that have been repeatedly vandalized

13.____

14. The Board of Education has a strong commitment to recreation.
Its recreation program focuses CHIEFLY on
    A. adult education programs in adult centers
    B. children and youth in after-school and evening centers
    C. the categories of pre-school, mentally handicapped, and senior citizens
    D. youth either considered to be pre-delinquent or adjudicated as delinquent

14.____

15. Those working to provide recreation to persons who have a physical, mental, emotional, or social disability frequently seek assistance from social service agencies.
Which of the following pairs of agencies is LEAST likely to be helpful to them?
    A. Catholic Charities; Federation of Protestant Welfare Agencies
    B. United Cerebral Palsy of N.Y.C.; New York Association for the Blind
    C. New York Association for Retarded Children; National Wheelchair Athletic Association
    D. New York League for Crippled and Disabled Children, Adults and Aging; Handclasp for the Handicapped, Inc.

15.____

16. Throughout the nation, there has been an increase in senior centers for aging persons.
Which of the following agencies does NOT sponsor special centers for aging persons?
    A. Housing Authority's low-income projects
    B. Office of Continuing Education
    C. Parks, Recreation and Cultural Affairs Administration
    D. Department of Social Services

16.____

17. The municipal department that has the PRIMARY responsibility for providing social services for youth, including recreation, is the
    A. Youth Activities Board
    B. Youth Services Agency
    C. United Block Association for Youth
    D. Bureau of Youth Community Services

17.____

18. If a recreation center director had severe problems with drug users in his neighborhood, the APPROPRIATE municipal department for him to ask for assistance is the
    A. Health and Hospitals Corporation
    B. Syanon or Phoenix House
    C. Department of Correction
    D. Addiction Services Agency

18.____

Questions 19-20.

DIRECTIONS: Questions 19 and 20 are to be answered SOLELY on the basis of the following passage.

This country was built on the puritanical belief that honest toil was the foundation of moral rectitude, the cement of society, and the uphill road to progress. Idleness was sin. As a result, we treat free time today as a conditional joy. We permit ourselves to relax only as a reward for hard work or as the recreation needed to put us back into shape for the job. Thus, the aimless delightful play of children gives way in adult life to a serious dedication to golf, the game that is so good for business.

19. According to the above passage, during former times in this country, respectable work was considered to be MOST NEARLY a
    A. way to improve health
    B. form of recreation
    C. developer of good character
    D. reward for leisure

19.____

20. According to the point of view presented in the above passage, it would be MOST reasonable to assume that an employer would consider an employee's vacation to be a time for the employee to
    A. determine his own leisure time priorities
    B. loaf and relax
    C. learn new recreational skills
    D. increase his effectiveness at work

20.____

Questions 21-23.

DIRECTIONS: Questions 21 through 23 are to be answered SOLELY on the basis of the following passage.

One of the key supervisory problems in a large municipal recreation department is that many leaders are assigned to isolated playgrounds or small centers, where it is difficult to observe their work regularly. Often their facilities are extremely limited. In such settings, as well as in larger recreation centers, where many recreation leaders tend to have other jobs as well, there tends to be a low level of morale and incentive. Still, it is the supervisor's task to help recreation personnel to develop pride in their work, and to maintain a high level of performance. With isolated leaders, the supervisor may give advice or assistance. Leaders may be assigned to different tasks or settings during the year to maximize their productivity and provide new challenges. When it is clear that leaders are not willing to make a real effort to contribute to the department, the possibility of penalties must be considered, within the scope of departmental policy and the union contract. However, the supervisor should be constructive, encourage and assist workers to take a greater interest in their work, be innovative, and try to raise morale and to improve performance in positive ways.

21. The one of the following that would be the MOST appropriate title for the foregoing passage is
    A. SMALL COMMUNITY CENTERS – PRO AND CON
    B. PLANNING BETTER RECREATION PROGRAMS
    C. THE SUPERVISOR'S TASK IN UPGRADING PERSONNEL PERFORMANCE
    D. THE SUPERVISOR AND THE MUNICIPAL UNION – RIGHTS AND OBLIGATIONS

21.____

22. The above passage makes clear that recreation leadership performance in ALL recreation playgrounds and centers throughout a large city is
    A. generally above average, with good morale on the part of most recreation leaders
    B. beyond description since no one has ever observed or evaluated leaders
    C. a key test of the personnel department's effort to develop more effective hiring standards
    D. of mixed quality, with many recreation leaders having poor morale and a low level of achievement

22.____

23. According to the above passage, the supervisor's role is to
    A. use disciplinary action as his major tool in upgrading performance
    B. tolerate the lack of effort of individual employees since they are assigned to isolated playgrounds or small centers
    C. employ encouragement, advice, and, when appropriate, disciplinary action to improve performance
    D. inform the county supervisor whenever malfeasance or idleness is detected

23.____

Questions 24-25.

DIRECTIONS: Questions 24 and 25 are to be answered SOLELY on the basis of the following passage.

A recent study revealed some very concrete evidence concerning the relationship between avocations and mental health. A number of well-adjusted persons were surveyed as to the type, number, and duration of their hobbies. The findings were compared to those from a similar survey of mentally disturbed persons. In the well-adjusted group, both the number of hobbies and the intensity with which they were pursued were far greater than that of the mentally disturbed group.

24. According to the above passage, the study showed that
    A. well-adjusted people engage in hobbies more widely and deeply than do mentally disturbed people
    B. hobbies, if taken seriously, serve to keep most people mentally well

24.____

C. mental patients should be taught hobbies as a part of their therapy
D. the degree of interest in hobbies plays an important role in maintaining good mental health

25. In reference to the study mentioned in the above passage, it is MOST accurate to say that it appears to have 25.____
    A. been based on a carefully-structured, complex research design
    B. considered the variables of mental health and hobby involvement
    C. contained a general definition of mental health
    D. given evidence of a causal relationship between hobbies and mental health

KEY (CORRECT ANSWERS)

1.	D	11.	C
2.	A	12.	A
3.	A	13.	D
4.	D	14.	B
5.	D	15.	D
6.	B	16.	B
7.	A	17.	B
8.	C	18.	D
9.	B	19.	C
10.	A	20.	D

21. C
22. D
23. C
24. A
25. B

RECORD KEEPING
EXAMINATION SECTION
TEST 1

DIRECTIONS: Each question or incomplete statement is followed by several suggested answers or completions. Select the one that BEST answers the question or completes the statement. *PRINT THE LETTER OF THE CORRECT ANSWER IN THE SPACE AT THE RIGHT.*

Questions 1-7.

DIRECTIONS: In answering Questions 1 through 7, use the following master list. For each question, determine where the name would fit on the master list. Each answer choice indicates right before or after the name in the answer choice.

> Aaron, Jane
> Armstead, Brendan
> Bailey, Charles
> Dent, Ricardo
> Grant, Mark
> Mars, Justin
> Methieu, Justine
> Parker, Cathy
> Sampson, Suzy
> Thomas, Heather

1. Schmidt, William
   A. Right before Cathy Parker
   B. Right after Heather Thomas
   C. Right after Suzy Sampson
   D. Right before Ricardo Dent

2. Asanti, Kendall
   A. Right before Jane Aaron
   B. Right after Charles Bailey
   C. Right before Justine Methieu
   D. Right after Brendan Armstead

3. O'Brien, Daniel
   A. Right after Justine Methieu
   B. Right before Jane Aaron
   C. Right after Mark Grant
   D. Right before Suzy Sampson

4. Marrow, Alison
   A. Right before Cathy Parker
   B. Right before Justin Mars
   C. Right before Mark Grant
   D. Right after Heather Thomas

5. Grantt, Marissa
   A. Right before Mark Grant
   B. Right after Mark Grant
   C. Right after Justin Mars
   D. Right before Suzy Sampson

1.____

2.____

3.____

4.____

5.____

69

6. Thompson, Heath   6.____
   A. Right after Justin Mars   B. Right before Suzy Sampson
   C. Right after Heather Thomas   D. Right before Cathy Parker

DIRECTIONS: Before answering Question 7, add in all of the names from Questions 1 through 6. Then fit the name in alphabetical order based on the new list.

7. Francisco, Mildred   7.____
   A. Right before Mark Grant   B. Right after Marissa Grantt
   C. Right before Alison Marrow   D. Right after Kendall Asanti

Questions 8-10.

DIRECTIONS: In answering Questions 8 through 10, compare each pair of names and addresses. Indicate whether they are the same or different in any way.

8. William H. Pratt, J.D.   William H. Pratt, J.D.   8.____
   Attourney at Law   Attorney at Law
   A. No differences   B. 1 difference
   C. 2 differences   D. 3 differences

9. 1303 Theater Drive,; Apt. 3-B   1330 Theatre Drive,; Apt. 3-B   9.____
   A. No differences   B. 1 difference
   C. 2 differences   D. 3 differences

10. Petersdorff, Briana and Mary   Petersdorff, Briana and Mary   10.____
    A. No differences   B. 1 difference
    C. 2 differences   D. 3 differences

11. Which of the following words, if any, are misspelled?   11.____
    A. Affordable   B. Circumstansial
    C. Legalese   D. None of the above

Questions 12-13.

DIRECTIONS: Questions 12 and 13 are to be answered on the basis of the following table.

Standardized Test Results for High School Students in District #1230

	English	Math	Science	Reading
High School 1	21	22	15	18
High School 2	12	16	13	15
High School 3	16	18	21	17
High School 4	19	14	15	16

The scores for each high school in the district were averaged out and listed for each subject tested. Scores of 0-10 are significantly below College Readiness Standards. 11-15 are below College Readiness, 16-20 meet College Readiness, and 21-25 are above College Readiness.

12. If the high schools need to meet or exceed in at least half the categories in order to NOT be considered "at risk," which schools are considered "at risk"? 12.____
   A. High School 2
   B. High School 3
   C. High School 4
   D. Both A and C

13. What percentage of subjects did the district as a whole meet or exceed College Readiness standards? 13.____
   A. 25%   B. 50%   C. 75%   D. 100%

Questions 14-15.

DIRECTIONS: Questions 14 and 15 are to be answered on the basis of the following information.

You have seven employees working as a part of your team: Austin, Emily, Jeremy, Christina, Martin, Harriet, and Steve. You have just sent an e-mail informing them that there will be a mandatory training session next week. To ensure that work still gets done, you are offering the training twice during the week: once on Tuesday and also on Thursday. This way half the employees will still be working while the other half attend the training. The only other issue is that Jeremy doesn't work on Tuesdays and Harriet doesn't work on Thursdays due to compressed work schedules.

14. Which of the following is a possible attendance roster for the first training session? 14.____
   A. Emily, Jeremy, Steve
   B. Steve, Christina, Harriet
   C. Harriet, Jeremy, Austin
   D. Steve, Martin, Jeremy

15. If Harriet, Christina, and Steve attend the training session on Tuesday, which of the following is a possible roster for Thursday's training session? 15.____
   A. Jeremy, Emily, and Austin
   B. Emily, Martin, and Harriet
   C. Austin, Christina, and Emily
   D. Jeremy, Emily, and Steve

Questions 16-20.

DIRECTIONS: In answering Questions 16 through 20, you will be given a word and will need to choose the answer choice that is MOST similar or different to the word.

16. Which word means the SAME as *annual*? 16.____
   A. Monthly   B. Usually   C. Yearly   D. Constantly

17. Which word means the SAME as *effort*? 17.____
   A. Energy   B. Equate   C. Cherish   D. Commence

18. Which word means the OPPOSITE of *forlorn*? 18.____
   A. Neglected   B. Lethargy   C. Optimistic   D. Astonished

19. Which word means the SAME as *risk*? 19.____
   A. Admire   B. Hazard   C. Limit   D. Hesitant

20. Which word means the OPPOSITE of *translucent*?
    A. Opaque
    B. Transparent
    C. Luminous
    D. Introverted

21. Last year, Jamie's annual salary was $50,000. Her boss called her today to inform her that she would receive a 20% raise for the upcoming year. How much more money will Jamie receive next year?
    A. $60,000
    B. $10,000
    C. $1,000
    D. $51,000

22. You and a co-worker work for a temp hiring agency as part of their office staff. You both are given 6 days off per month. How many days off are you and your co-worker given in a year?
    A. 24
    B. 72
    C. 144
    D. 48

23. If Margot makes $34,000 per year and she works 40 hours per week for all 52 weeks, what is her hourly rate?
    A. $16.34/hour
    B. $17.00/hour
    C. $15.54/hour
    D. $13.23/hour

24. How many dimes are there in $175.00?
    A. 175
    B. 1,750
    C. 3,500
    D. 17,500

25. If Janey is three times as old as Emily, and Emily is 3, how old is Janey?
    A. 6
    B. 9
    C. 12
    D. 15

KEY (CORRECT ANSWERS)

1.	C		11.	B
2.	D		12.	A
3.	A		13.	D
4.	B		14.	B
5.	B		15.	A
6.	C		16.	C
7.	A		17.	A
8.	B		18.	C
9.	C		19.	B
10.	A		20.	A

21. B
22. C
23. A
24. B
25. B

TEST 2

DIRECTIONS: Each question or incomplete statement is followed by several suggested answers or completions. Select the one that BEST answers the question or completes the statement. *PRINT THE LETTER OF THE CORRECT ANSWER IN THE SPACE AT THE RIGHT.*

Questions 1-6.

DIRECTIONS: Questions 1 through 6 are to be answered on the basis of the following information.

item	name of item to be ordered
quantity	minimum number that can be ordered
beginning amount	amount in stock at start of month
amount received	amount receiving during month
ending amount	amount in stock at end of month
amount used	amount used during month
amount to order	will need at least as much of each item as used in the previous month
unit price	cost of each unit of an item
total price	total price for the order

Item	Quantity	Beginning	Received	Ending	Amount Used	Amount to Order	Unit Price	Total Price
Pens	10	22	10	8	24	20	$0.11	$2.20
Spiral notebooks	8	30	13	12			$0.25	
Binder clips	2 boxes	3 boxes	1 box	1 box			$1.79	
Sticky notes	3 packs	12 packs	4 packs	2 packs			$1.29	
Dry erase markers	1 pack (dozen)	34 markers	8 markers	40 markers			$16.49	
Ink cartridges (printer)	1 cartridge	3 cartridges	1 cartridge	2 cartridges			$79.99	
Folders	10 folders	25 folders	15 folders	10 folders			$1.08	

1. How many packs of sticky notes were used during the month?   1._____
   A. 16   B. 10   C. 12   D. 14

2. How many folders need to be ordered for next month?   2._____
   A. 15   B. 20   C. 30   D. 40

3. What is the total price of notebooks that you will need to order?   3._____
   A. $6.00   B. $0.25   C. $4.50   D. $2.75

4. Which of the following will you spend the second most money on?   4._____
   A. Ink cartridges   B. Dry erase markers
   C. Sticky notes   D. Binder clips

5. How many packs of dry erase markers should you order?   5._____
   A. 1   B. 8   C. 12   D. 0

6. What will be the total price of the file folders you order? 6._____
   A. $20.16   B. $21.60   C. $10.80   D. $4.32

Questions 7-11.

DIRECTIONS: Questions 7 through 11 are to be answered on the basis of the following table.

Number of Car Accidents, By Location and Cause, for 2014						
	Location 1		Location 2		Location 3	
Cause	Number	Percent	Number	Percent	Number	Percent
Severe Weather	10		25		30	
Excessive Speeding	20	40	5		10	
Impaired Driving	15		15	25	8	
Miscellaneous	5		15		2	4
TOTALS	50	100	60	100	50	100

7. Which of the following is the third highest cause of accidents for all three locations? 7._____
   A. Severe Weather   B. Impaired Driving
   C. Miscellaneous   D. Excessive Speeding

8. The average number of Severe Weather accidents per week at Location 3 for the year (52 weeks) was MOST NEARLY 8._____
   A. 0.57   B. 30   C. 1   D. 1.25

9. Which location had the LARGEST percentage of accidents caused by Impaired Driving? 9._____
   A. 1   B. 2   C. 3   D. Both A and B

10. If one-third of the accidents at all three locations resulted in at least one fatality, what is the LEAST amount of deaths caused by accidents last year? 10._____
    A. 60   B. 106   C. 66   D. 53

11. What is the percentage of accidents caused by miscellaneous means from all three locations in 2014? 11._____
    A. 5%   B. 10%   C. 13%   D. 25%

12. How many pairs of the following groups of letters are exactly alike? 12._____
    ACDOBJ   ACDBOJ
    HEWBWR   HEWRWB
    DEERVS   DEERVS
    BRFQSX   BRFQSX
    WEYRVB   WEYRVB
    SPQRZA   SQRPZA

    A. 2   B. 3   C. 4   D. 5

3 (#2)

Questions 13-19.

DIRECTIONS: Questions 13 through 19 are to be answered on the basis of the following information.

In 2012, the most current information on the American population was finished. The information was compiled by 200 volunteers in each of the 50 states. The territory of Puerto Rico, a sovereign of the United States, had 25 people assigned to compile data. In February of 2010, volunteers in each state and sovereign began collecting information. In Puerto Rico, data collection finished by January 31st, 2011, while work in the United States was completed on June 30, 2012. Each volunteer gathered data on the population of their state or sovereign. When the information was compiled, volunteers sent reports to the nation's capital, Washington, D.C. Each volunteer worked 20 hours per month and put together 10 reports per month. After the data was compiled in total, 50 people reviewed the data and worked from January 2012 to December 2012.

13. How many reports were generated from February 2010 to April 2010 in Illinois and Ohio?   13._____
    A. 3,000   B. 6,000   C. 12,000   D. 15,000

14. How many volunteers in total collected population data in January 2012?   14._____
    A. 10,000   B. 2,000   C. 225   D. 200

15. How many reports were put together in May 2012?   15._____
    A. 2,000   B. 50,000   C. 100,000   D. 100,250

16. How many hours did the Puerto Rican volunteers work in the fall (September-November)?   16._____
    A. 60   B. 500   C. 1,500   D. 0

17. How many workers were compiling or reviewing data in July 2012?   17._____
    A. 25   B. 50   C. 200   D. 250

18. What was the total amount of hours worked by Nevada volunteers in July 2010?   18._____
    A. 500   B. 4,000   C. 4,500   D. 5,000

19. How many reviewers worked in January 2013?   19._____
    A. 75   B. 50   C. 0   D. 25

20. John has to file 10 documents per shelf. How many documents would it take for John to fill 40 shelves?   20._____
    A. 40   B. 400   C. 4,500   D. 5,000

21. Jill wants to travel from New York City to Los Angeles by bike, which is approximately 2,772 miles. How many miles per day would Jill need to average if she wanted to complete the trip in 4 weeks?   21._____
    A. 100   B. 89   C. 99   D. 94

4 (#2)

22. If there are 24 CPU's and only 7 monitors, how many more monitors do you need to have the same amount of monitors as CPU's?
    A. Not enough information   B. 17
    C. 31   D. 0

22.____

23. If Gerry works 5 days a week and 8 hours each day, and John works 3 days a week and 10 hours each day, how many more hours per year will Gerry work than John?
    A. They work the same amount of hours.
    B. 450
    C. 520
    D. 832

23.____

24. Jimmy gets transferred to a new office. The new office has 25 employees, but only 16 are there due to a blizzard. How many coworkers was Jimmy able to meet on his first day?
    A. 16   B. 25   C. 9   D. 7

24.____

25. If you do a fundraiser for charities in your area and raise $500 total, how much would you give to each charity if you were donating equal amounts to 3 of them?
    A. $250.00   B. $167.77   C. $50.00   D. $111.11

25.____

KEY (CORRECT ANSWERS)

1.	D		11.	C
2.	B		12.	B
3.	A		13.	C
4.	C		14.	A
5.	D		15.	C
6.	B		16.	C
7.	D		17.	B
8.	A		18.	B
9.	A		19.	C
10.	D		20.	B

21. C
22. B
23. C
24. A
25. B

TEST 3

DIRECTIONS: Each question or incomplete statement is followed by several suggested answers or completions. Select the one that BEST answers the question or completes the statement. *PRINT THE LETTER OF THE CORRECT ANSWER IN THE SPACE AT THE RIGHT.*

Questions 1-3.

DIRECTIONS: In answering Questions 1 through 3, choose the correctly spelled word.

1. A. allusion B. alusion C. allusien D. allution 1.____

2. A. altitude B. alltitude C. atlitude D. altltude 2.____

3. A. althogh B. allthough C. althrough D. although 3.____

Questions 4-9.

DIRECTIONS: In answering Questions 4 through 9, choose the answer that BEST completes the analogy.

4. Odometer is to mileage as compass is to 4.____
   A. speed B. needle C. hiking D. direction

5. Marathon is to race as hibernation is to 5.____
   A. winter B. dream C. sleep D. bear

6. Cup is to coffee as bowl is to 6.____
   A. dish B. spoon C. food D. soup

7. Flow is to river as stagnant is to 7.____
   A. pool B. rain C. stream D. canal

8. Paw is to cat as hoof is to 8.____
   A. lamb B. horse C. lion D. elephant

9. Architect is to building as sculptor is to 9.____
   A. museum B. chisel C. stone D. statue

Questions 10-14.

DIRECTIONS: Questions 10 through 14 are to be answered on the basis of the following graph.

Population of Carroll City Broken Down by Age and Gender (in Thousands)			
Age	Female	Male	Total
Under 15	60	60	120
15-23		22	
24-33		20	44
34-43	13	18	31
44-53	20		67
64 and Over	65	65	130
TOTAL	230	232	462

10. How many people in the city are between the ages of 15-23?
    A. 70   B. 46,000   C. 70,000   D. 225,000

11. Approximately what percentage of the total population of the city was female aged 24-33?
    A. 10%   B. 5%   C. 15%   D. 25%

12. If 33% of the males have a job and 55% of females don't have a job, which of the following statements is TRUE?
    A. Males have approximately 2,600 more jobs than females.
    B. Females have approximately 49,000 more jobs than males.
    C. Females have approximately 26,000 more jobs than males.
    D. None of the above statements are true.

13. How many females between the ages of 15-23 live in Carroll City?
    A. 67,000   B. 24,000   C. 48,000   D. 91,000

14. Assume all males 44-53 living in Carroll City are employed. If two-thirds of males age 44-53 work jobs outside of Carroll City, how many work within city limits?
    A. 31,333
    B. 15,667
    C. 47,000
    D. Cannot answer the question with the information provided

10.____

11.____

12.____

13.____

14.____

Questions 15-16.

DIRECTIONS: Questions 15 and 16 are labeled as shown. Alphabetize them for filing. Choose the answer that correctly shows the order.

15. (1) AED
    (2) OOS
    (3) FOA
    (4) DOM
    (5) COB

    A. 2-5-4-3-2   B. 1-4-5-2-3   C. 1-5-4-2-3   D. 1-5-4-3-2

15.____

16. Alphabetize the names of the people. Last names are given last.
    (1) Lindsey Jamestown
    (2) Jane Alberta
    (3) Ally Jamestown
    (4) Allison Johnston
    (5) Lyle Moreno

    A. 2-1-3-4-5   B. 3-4-2-1-5   C. 2-3-1-4-5   D. 4-3-2-1-5

16.____

17. Which of the following words is misspelled?
    A. disgust
    B. whisper
    C. locale
    D. none of the above

17.____

Questions 18-21.

DIRECTIONS: Questions 18 through 21 are to be answered on the basis of the following list of employees.

Robertson, Aaron
Bacon, Gina
Jerimiah, Trace
Gillette, Stanley
Jacks, Sharon

18. Which employee name would come in third in alphabetized list?
    A. Robertson, Aaron
    B. Jerimiah, Trace
    C. Gillette, Stanley
    D. Jacks, Sharon

18.____

19. Which employee's first name starts with the letter in the alphabet that is five letters after the first letter of their last name?
    A. Jerimiah, Trace
    B. Bacon, Gina
    C. Jacks, Sharon
    D. Gillette, Stanley

19.____

20. How many employees have last names that are exactly five letters long?
    A. 1   B. 2   C. 3   D. 4

20.____

21. How many of the employees have either a first or last name that starts with the letter "G"? 21.____
 A. 1 B. 2 C. 4 D. 5

Questions 22-25.

DIRECTIONS: Questions 22 through 25 are to be answered on the basis of the following chart.

Bicycle Sales (Model #34JA32)							
Country	May	June	July	August	September	October	Total
Germany	34	47	45	54	56	60	296
Britain	40	44	36	47	47	46	260
Ireland	37	32	32	32	34	33	200
Portugal	14	14	14	16	17	14	89
Italy	29	29	28	31	29	31	177
Belgium	22	24	24	26	25	23	144
Total	176	198	179	206	208	207	1166

22. What percentage of the overall total was sold to the German importer? 22.____
 A. 25.3% B. 22% C. 24.1% D. 23%

23. What percentage of the overall total was sold in September? 23.____
 A. 24.1% B. 25.6% C. 17.9% D. 24.6%

24. What is the average number of units per month imported into Belgium over the first four months shown? 24.____
 A. 26 B. 20 C. 24 D. 31

25. If you look at the three smallest importers, what is their total import percentage? 25.____
 A. 35.1% B. 37.1% C. 40% D. 28%

KEY (CORRECT ANSWERS)

1. A
2. A
3. D
4. D
5. C

6. D
7. A
8. B
9. D
10. C

11. B
12. C
13. C
14. B
15. D

16. C
17. D
18. D
19. B
20. B

21. B
22. A
23. C
24. C
25. A

TEST 4

DIRECTIONS: Each question or incomplete statement is followed by several suggested answers or completions. Select the one that BEST answers the question or completes the statement. *PRINT THE LETTER OF THE CORRECT ANSWER IN THE SPACE AT THE RIGHT.*

Questions 1-6.

DIRECTIONS: In answering Questions 1 through 6, choose the sentence that represents the BEST example of English grammar.

1.
   A. Joey and me want to go on a vacation next week.
   B. Gary told Jim he would need to take some time off.
   C. If turning six years old, Jim's uncle would teach Spanish to him.
   D. Fax a copy of your resume to Ms. Perez and me.

   1.____

2.
   A. Jerry stood in line for almost two hours.
   B. The reaction to my engagement was less exciting than I thought it would be.
   C. Carlos and me have done great work on this project.
   D. Two parts of the speech needs to be revised before tomorrow.

   2.____

3.
   A. Arriving home, the alarm was tripped.
   B. Jonny is regarded as a stand up guy, a responsible parent, and he doesn't give up until a task is finished.
   C. Each employee must submit a drug test each month.
   D. One of the documents was incinerated in the explosion.

   3.____

4.
   A. As soon as my parents get home, I told them I finished all of my chores.
   B. I asked my teacher to send me my missing work, check my absences, and how did I do on my test.
   C. Matt attempted to keep it concealed from Jenny and me.
   D. If Mary or him cannot get work done on time, I will have to split them up.

   4.____

5.
   A. Driving to work, the traffic report warned him of an accident on Highway 47.
   B. Jimmy has performed well this season.
   C. Since finishing her degree, several job offers have been given to Cam.
   D. Our boss is creating unstable conditions for we employees.

   5.____

6.
   A. The thief was described as a tall man with a wiry mustache weighing approximately 150 pounds.
   B. She gave Patrick and I some more time to finish our work.
   C. One of the books that he ordered was damaged in shipping.
   D. While talking on the rotary phone, the car Jim was driving skidded off the road.

   6.____

Questions 7-9.

DIRECTIONS: Questions 7 through 9 are to be answered on the basis of the following graph.

Ice Lake Frozen Flight (2002-2013)		
Year	Number of Participants	Temperature (Fahrenheit)
2002	22	4°
2003	50	33°
2004	69	18°
2005	104	22°
2006	108	24°
2007	288	33°
2008	173	9°
2009	598	39°
2010	698	26°
2011	696	30°
2012	777	28°
2013	578	32°

7. Which two year span had the LARGEST difference between temperatures?
   A. 2002 and 2003
   B. 2011 and 2012
   C. 2008 and 2009
   D. 2003 and 2004

8. How many total people participated in the years after the temperature reached at least 29°?
   A. 2,295   B. 1,717   C. 2,210   D. 4,543

9. In 2007, the event saw 288 participants, while in 2008 that number dropped to 173. Which of the following reasons BEST explains the drop in participants?
   A. The event had not been going on that long and people didn't know about it.
   B. The lake water wasn't cold enough to have people jump in.
   C. The temperature was too cold for many people who would have normally participated.
   D. None of the above reasons explain the drop in participants.

10. In the following list of numbers, how many times does 4 come just after 2 when 2 comes just after an odd number?
    2365247653898632488572486392424
    A. 2   B. 3   C. 4   D. 5

11. Which choice below lists the letter that is as far after B as S is after N in the alphabet?
    A. G   B. H   C. I   D. J

Questions 12-15.

DIRECTIONS: Questions 12 through 15 are to be answered on the basis of the following directory and list of changes.

Directory		
Name	Emp. Type	Position
Julie Taylor	Warehouse	Packer
James King	Office	Administrative Assistant
John Williams	Office	Salesperson
Ray Moore	Warehouse	Maintenance
Kathleen Byrne	Warehouse	Supervisor
Amy Jones	Office	Salesperson
Paul Jonas	Office	Salesperson
Lisa Wong	Warehouse	Loader
Eugene Lee	Office	Accountant
Bruce Lavine	Office	Manager
Adam Gates	Warehouse	Packer
Will Suter	Warehouse	Packer
Gary Lorper	Office	Accountant
Jon Adams	Office	Salesperson
Susannah Harper	Office	Salesperson

Directory Updates:
- Employee e-mail addresses will adhere to the following guidelines: lastnamefirstname@apexindustries.com (ex. Susannah Harper is harpersusannah@apexindustries.com). Currently, employees in the warehouse share one e-mail, distribution@apexindustries.com.
- The "Loader" position will now be referred to as "Specialist I"
- Adam Gates has accepted a Supervisor position within the Warehouse and is no longer a Packer. All warehouse employees report to the two Supervisors and all office employees report to the Manager.

12. Amy Jones tried to send an e-mail to Adam Gates, but it wouldn't send. Which of the following offers the BEST explanation?
    A. Amy put Adam's first name first and then his last name.
    B. Adam doesn't check his e-mail, so he wouldn't know if he received the e-mail or not.
    C. Adam does not have his own e-mail.
    D. Office employees are not allowed to send e-mails to each other.

13. How many Packers currently work for Apex Industries?
    A. 2   B. 3   C. 4   D. 5

14. What position does Lisa Wong currently hold?
    A. Specialist I
    B. Secretary
    C. Administrative Assistant
    D. Loader

15. If an employee wanted to contact the office manager, which of the following e-mails should the e-mail be sent to? 15.____
    A. officemanager@apexindustries.com
    B. brucelavine@apexindustries.com
    C. lavinebruce@apexindustries.com
    D. distribution@apexindustries.com

Questions 16-19.

DIRECTIONS: In answering Questions 16 through 19, compare the three names, numbers or addresses.

16. Smiley Yarnell   Smiley Yarnel   Smily Yarnell   16.____
    A. All three are exactly alike.
    B. The first and second are exactly alike.
    C. The second and third are exactly alike.
    D. All three are different.

17. 1583 Theater Drive   1583 Theater Drive   1583 Theatre Drive   17.____
    A. All three are exactly alike.
    B. The first and second are exactly alike.
    C. The second and third are exactly alike.
    D. All three are different.

18. 3341893212   3341893212   3341893212   18.____
    A. All three are exactly alike.
    B. The first and second are exactly alike.
    C. The second and third are exactly alike.
    D. All three are different.

19. Douglass Watkins   Douglas Watkins   Douglass Watkins   19.____
    A. All three are exactly alike.
    B. The first and third are exactly alike.
    C. The second and third are exactly alike.
    D. All three are different.

Questions 20-24.

DIRECTIONS: In answering Questions 20 through 24, you will be presented with a word. Choose the synonym that BEST represents the word in question.

20. Flexible   20.____
    A. delicate   B. inflammable   C. strong   D. pliable

21. Alternative   21.____
    A. choice   B. moderate   C. lazy   D. value

22. Corroborate
    A. examine   B. explain   C. verify   D. explain   22.____

23. Respiration
    A. recovery   B. breathing   C. sweating   D. selfish   23.____

24. Negligent
    A. lazy   B. moderate   C. hopeless   D. lax   24.____

25. Plumber is to Wrench as Painter is to
    A. pipe   B. shop   C. hammer   D. brush   25.____

KEY (CORRECT ANSWERS)

1.	D	11.	A
2.	A	12.	C
3.	D	13.	A
4.	C	14.	A
5.	B	15.	C
6.	C	16.	D
7.	C	17.	B
8.	B	18.	A
9.	C	19.	B
10.	C	20.	D

21. A
22. C
23. B
24. D
25. D

BASIC FUNDAMENTALS OF SPORTS

CONTENTS

	Page
PRINCIPLES OF ATHLETICS	1
BASKETBALL	1
CROSS-COUNTRY AND DISTANCE RUNNING	4
SOCCER	8
SOFTBALL	11
SPEEDBALL	14
TOUCH FOOTBALL	18
VOLLEYBALL	23

BASIC FUNDAMENTALS OF SPORTS

PRINCIPLES OF ATHLETICS

ATHLETICS IN THE PHYSICAL TRAINING PROGRAM

- ❖ Athletics deserve a prominent place in the physical training program because they contribute to the increased efficiency of the student. Because of the competitive nature of athletics and their natural appeal, the students take part in them with enthusiasm. Athletic teams formed at the intramural and higher levels are a strong unifying influence and provide one of the best means of developing esprit de corps.

- ❖ The athletic sports selected must be vigorous to insure good conditioning value.

- ❖ All the components of physical fitness cannot be developed with athletics alone. These sports are beneficial primarily in sustaining interest in the program and maintaining a level of physical fitness. Therefore, athletics are to be considered as a supplement and not a substitute for the less interest conditioning drills.

BASKETBALL

INTRODUCTION

Basketball has enjoyed increased popularity and growth within the past few years, unequaled by any other American sport. It should be comparatively easy for an instructor to create interest in basketball among student personnel, both for conditioning and recreational purposes. Few sports have the potentialities that basketball has for developing coordination, endurance, skill, teamwork, and the will to win. It is an excellent activity for the sustaining stage. One of the objectives of a physical training program is 100 percent participation. A well-organized basketball program makes it possible to more nearly accomplish this objective than any other athletic activity.

BASIC SKILLS

Men prefer to play rather than practice so, whenever possible, a part of each instruction period should be devoted to a scrimmage game. To prevent the loss of program interest, the instructor should vary the practice routine, add new plays, organize tournaments, and devise other ways to maintain enthusiasm. He should use textbooks written by professional basketball coaches to plan and teach offensive and defensive plays.

    A. Fundamentals

        1. Shooting Baskets
           a. One-hand Set Shots: Shoot from a balanced position. Keep both feet on the floor. Follow through.
           b. Two-hand Set Shots: Shoot from a balanced position and apply equal pressure on the ball with each hand. Keep both feet on the floor. Follow through.

c. Lay-ups: Jump high, reach high before releasing the ball. Spin the ball, using the backboard when possible.
d. Shooting while on move. This is usually a one-handed shot. Shoot off opposite foot from the hand that releases the ball.
e. Jump Shot: Jump high, release ball with one hand at apex of height. Most common shot today.
f. Free Throws: These are one-hand and two-hand underhand throws and two-hand push shots. Put a slight back spin on the ball.

2. Ball-handling.
   a. Two-hand Chest Pass: Step in the direction of the pass. Use a wrist action to release the ball with a back spin.
   b. One-hand and Two-hand Bounce Pass: Step in the direction of the pass. Bounce the ball a reasonable distance in front of the receiver, putting a back spin on the ball with a wrist action.
   c. One-hand Baseball Pass: Step in the direction of the pass; throw as you would throw a baseball. This is used mostly for long passes.
   d. Two-hand Overhead Pass: Hold the ball above the head with the arms extended. Throw with a wrist action. This pass is used mainly to get the ball to the pivot man who is close to the basket.

3. Dribbling
   a. Changing Hand With Ball: Only one hand may touch the ball at one time while dribbling. The hand may be alternated.
   b. Change of Pace: Changing speed and direction while dribbling.
   c. Dribbling Exercise With Eyes Not Directly On Ball: Change direction; change hand; keep the head up with the eyes directed toward possible passing or shooting situations.

4. Footwork
   a. Pivoting: Give the pivotman or center special practice in pivoting. One foot remains stationary while the opposite foot is mobile.
   b. Individual Defense: Stress footwork and the position of the hands and body.
   c. Check Position of Feet When Shooting Various Types of Shots: Points to check: the position of balance; correct foot forward when in shooting position; the distance between each foot.

B. Small Group or Team Practice

1. Man-to-Man Defense
   a. Switching: Each defensive man is responsible for defending against a designated man, until a screen or block forces the defensive man to change defensive responsibility.
   b. Nonswitching: Each defensive man is responsible for a designated man with the defensive man going through or behind screens and blocks.

2. Man-to-man Offense: Various types of offensive formations have been especially designed to combat man-to-man defense. Use textbooks written by professional coaches for technical knowledge.

3. Zone Defense: There are numerous variations of this type defense aimed at defending a restricted area in front of the basket. The defensive target is the ball, not the man.

4. Zone Offense: The zone offense forces the defense to adjust position, as a unit, rapidly and often. Zone offense is most effective when employing rapid movement of the ball within the defense area.

5. Defense Against Fast Break: Stress rebound work on the offensive backboard. Stress court balance by offensive team.

6. Fast Break Offense: Move down court into scoring or offensive territory quickly.

PRACTICE DRILLS

Some practice routines are:

A. Keep-Away: Divide unit into two groups. Designate each individual's defensive responsibility by name or number. Use half of a basketball court as the playing area. The team in possession of the ball passes it among the team members until the defense gets possession of it. Basketball rules apply. Continue with each team taking turns as it gets possession of the ball.

B. Shooting Exercise: Divide unit into small groups. Each group has a ball. Designate the various positions on the floor where the shooting practice is to be done. Use a pre-arranged scoring method. Play numerous games, giving each group an opportunity to shoot from all positions on the floor.

C. Dribbling Exercise: Divide unit into two or three groups. Each group has a ball. Conduct a dribbling relay. Place obstacles for dribblers to avoid and designate the path each team will follow.

D. Defense Exercises: Use the two free throw circles and the restraining circle at center court. Place five men around the outside of each circle. One man is in the center of each ring. It is the job of the man in the center to intercept or deflect the path of the ball which is passed from man to man in the circle. When the man inside the circle succeeds in intercepting, deflecting, or touching the ball, the passer takes his place.

FACILITIES AND EQUIPMENT

A. Facilities: In some sections of the country, outdoor facilities may be used, and they are easily constructed. The minimum dimensions of a court for competition are approximately 74 feet by 42 feet; maximum dimensions are 94 feet by 50 feet.

B. Equipment: A basketball is the only required equipment. For highly organized competition, however, uniforms, special shoes, and other equipment may be required.

RULES

So-called college rules or, more correctly, The National Collegiate Athletic Association rules, are used in conducting basketball in the physical training program. Each year a new paper-bound guide booklet is published and sold by the NCAA.

CROSS-COUNTRY AND DISTANCE RUNNING

INTRODUCTION

A. Long-distance running gives some benefits that cannot be obtained in the same degree from any other sport. It builds powerful leg muscles, increases the long capacity, and develops endurance. For these reasons, cross-country and distance running should be included in the physical training program. These sports require only a few miles of open space that is available at school. They do require time, however, and many physical training supervisors do not find it feasible to use them as individual full-time sports. Short cross-country runs and middle-distance runs can be used to supplement other activities, particularly the team sports or the sports that develop precision or agility rather than endurance. Short cross-country runs can be scheduled once a week, gradually increasing the distance as the physical condition of the men improves; or distance running can be combined with other activities such as the conditioning exercises.

B. Cross-country and the distance runs do not enjoy equal popularity with other sports, for obvious reasons. They require great endurance, and endurance requires months of rigid training. There is a common belief that long-distance running is too strenuous, often resulting in permanent injury to the heart. While distance running may be harmful to the man who overdoses the sport, when he is not in proper physical condition, the conditioned, supervised distance runner is in no greater danger of strain than the man engaged in any other athletic activity.

LONG-DISTANCE RUNS

Any run over a mile is classified as a long-distance run. The instructor may vary the distance of the run during the season, or he may standardize it at whatever length will best suit his men or the facilities available to him. Two miles is the most popular distance. Often, the two-mile run is included as an event in track and field meets, but more frequently it is treated as a separate sport. The two-mile run may be run on any type of flat outdoor course, on a regular cinder track, or on a grass or dirt course. Because the ground is often frozen too hard for long-distance running during cold weather, the two-mile run is not recommended as a winter activity except in mild climates. The sport is too strenuous for very hot weather. The run cannot be held indoors. Constant pounding of the feet on the hard surface causes shin splints and injuries to the ankle joints.

CROSS-COUNTRY RUNS

Cross-country is a distance run held on a course laid out along roads, across fields, over hills, through woods, on any irregular ground. A flat cylinder or dirt track is not a suitable surface for cross-country running. Opinions vary as to the proper length of a cross-country course. Some runs are as long as six miles. Five miles used to be accepted as standard, but recently there has been a tendency to shorten the run to four or even three miles. Only if time is available for a full-season cross-country program should the physical training instructor try to train men for a five-mile course. If time is limited, or if cross-country running is being used to supplement other activities, the three-mile course is long enough for most men.

PLACE IN THE PROGRAM

Cross-country and distance running should be used only after the men reach the sustaining stage of conditioning. They should then be scheduled occasionally to provide variety in the program. Cross-country running has the advantage of allowing mass participation. Interest can be stimulated by putting the runs on a competitive basis.

BASIC SKILLS

A. Cross-Country Running Form: Running form in cross-country races varies with the terrain and the contour of the course. On the flat, use the same form as used in a two-mile run. The body lean should be between 5 and 10 percent. A lean of more than 10 percent places too much weight and strain on the legs. A lean of less than 5 percent is retarding. In running uphill, lean forward at a greater angle and cut the length of the stride. To gain an added lift, swing the arms high and bring the knees up high on each stride. Do not slow down after reaching the crest of the hill, but resume the flat course stride as soon as the ground levels off. The runner's stride will naturally lengthen in doing downhill, but he should not stretch his stride or increase his pace too much. There is less control and less balance when running downhill; therefore, there is greater danger of turning an ankle and of falling. Keep the arms low, swinging freely, and use them as a brake and as a balance. Coming onto the flat from a downhill run, do not slow down but float or coast into a flat course pace. More energy will be used in attempting to brake the speed of descent than in maintaining the faster pace and slowing down gradually. Run on the toes or the balls of the feet, rather than on the heels. Landing on the heels throughout a five-mile course would jolt the entire body injuriously. Runners who have a tendency to strike the heel on the ground should wear a cotton or sponge rubber pad in the heels of their shoes, unless their footgear has rubber heels.

B. Racing Tactics for Cross-Country

1. Teams can be pitted against each other in cross-country races. Certain members of the team may need encouragement along the way. If the team runs well-bunched for most of the course, the stronger runners can lead and encourage the weaker men. The pace should be scaled to the pace of the average runner on the team. Within a mile of the finish, however, the group should break and each man run out the race for himself.

2. If the coach prefers his team to run on an individual basis, there are several techniques for outwitting opponents. A good runner may not take the lead but stay behind an opponent and conserve his energy for the final sprint. The opponent may tire himself out trying to maintain the lead and become so discouraged when passed by a strong sprint near the finish line that he will not fight to reach the tape first. If leading an opponent, a runner may discourage him by constantly increasing the lead when he is out of sight. Opportunities for doing this frequently occur at corners of the course obscured by trees or bushes. If the leading runner sprints a short distance after rounding the corner, he may increase his lead 10 or 15 yards. After this has happened two or three times, an easily discouraged opponent may cease to be a serious contender for the race.

PRACTICE METHODS

A. Conditioning is more essential to distance and cross-country running than to any other sport. Championship distance running depends on stamina, and stamina can be developed only through constant training. A man of only average ability can become an outstanding distance runner by steady and careful training. Hiking is the best method for getting into condition before the season opens. Long walks build up leg muscles. During the first month of the season, training should be gradual, starting with short distances and increasing day by day. At first, the legs will become stiff, but the stiffness gradually disappears if running is practiced for a while every day. To prevent strain, it is essential to limber up thoroughly each day before running.

B. In the mass training of a large group, leaders should be stationed at the head and the rear of the column, and they should make every effort to keep the men together. After determining the abilities of the men in cross-country running, it is advisable to divide the unit into three groups. The poorest conditioned group is started first, the best conditioned group last. The starting time of the groups should be staggered so that all of them come in about the same time. In preliminary training, the running is similar to ordinary road work in that it begins with rather slow jogging, alternating with walking. The speed and distance of the run is gradually increased. As the condition of the men improves, occasional sprints may be introduced. At first, the distance run is from one-half to one mile. It is gradually increased to two or three miles. On completing the run, the men should be required to continue walking for three or four minutes before stopping, to permit a gradual cooling off and return to normal physiological functioning.

FACILITIES AND EQUIPMENT

A. A course three or five miles long should be measured and marked by one or the three methods specified below:

1. Directional arrows fastened to the top of a tall post and placed at every point where the course turns. Such signs should also be placed at ever other point where there may be doubt as to the direction of travel.

2. A lime line placed on the ground over the entire course.

3. Flags: they should be clearly visible to the runners.
    a. A red flag indicates a left turn.
    b. A white flag indicates a right turn.
    c. A blue flag indicates the course is straight ahead.

B. There should be at least one stopwatch (preferably three) for timing the runners.

RULES

A. Team Members: A cross-country team shall consist of seven men, unless otherwise agreed. In dual meets, a maximum of twelve men may be entered, but a maximum of seven shall enter into the scoring.

B. Scoring: First place shall score 1 point, second place 2, third place 3, and so on. All men who finish the course shall be ranked and tallied in this manner. The team score shall then be determined by totaling the points scored by the first five men of each team to finish. The team scoring the least number of points shall be the winner. Note: Although the sixth and seventh runners of a team to finish do not score points toward their team's total, it should be noted that their places, if better than those of any of the first five of an opposing team, serve to increase the team score of the opponents.

C. Cancellation of Points: If less than five (or the number determined prior to the race) finish, the places of all members of that team shall be disregarded.

D. Tie Event: In case the total points scored by two or more teams result in a tie, the event shall be called a tie.

8
SOCCER

INTRODUCTION

    A. Soccer is one of the best athletic activities for developing endurance, agility, leg strength, and a great degree of skill in using the legs. The game is the most popular sport in Europe and is the national game of many of the Central and South American countries. In recent years, it has become popular in United States schools and colleges.

    B. A soccer ball is the only equipment needed for the game, and the men can learn to play it easily. The men do not need much skill to participate, but the amount they can developed in unlimited.

PLACE IN THE PROGRAM

Soccer should be introduced into the physical training program during the latter part of the slow improvement stage and used as a competitive activity in the sustaining stage. It is primarily a spring or fall sport. Any level field is suitable for competition. The boundaries for the soccer field are similar to the dimensions for a football field. Goal posts are essential to the game, but they are easily constructed and are usually of a temporary nature, so that they may be removed when not in use.

BASIC SKILLS

    A. Passing: Passing with the feet is the basic means of moving the ball. Short passes are easier to control and can be done more accurately than long ones. Emphasis should be continually placed on skill in passing.

    B. Dribbling: The ball is dribbled by a series of kicks with the inside or outside of the foot. Do not kick with the toe. Keep the head over the ball when kicking and propel it only a short distance at a time. Keep it close to the feet. When the ball gets very far from the feet while dribbling, an opposing player can easily take it away.

    C. Instep Kicking: The instep kick, which is the basic soccer kick, is made from the knee joint instead of from the hip as in football. The toe does not come in contact with the ball. It is pointed downward and the instep (the shoe laces) is applied to the ball with a vigorous snap from the knee. For a stationary ball, the non-kicking foot is alongside the ball at the time of the kick. For a ball rolling toward the kicker, his non-kicking foot stops short of the ball; for a ball rolling away from the kicker, his non-kicking foot stops beyond the ball. The kicker must keep his eye on the ball until it has left his foot.

    D. Inside-of-the-Foot Kicking: The ball is kicked with the inside of the foot and the leg is swung from the hip. The toe is turned outward and the sole of the foot is parallel with the ground as the foot strikes the ball. The tall should be well under the body at the time of contact. This kick is used for short passes and for dribbling.

    E. Foot Trapping: The foot trap is the method of stopping the ball by trapping it between the ground and the foot. Place the sole of the foot on top of the ball at the instant it touches the ground, but do not stamp on it. Keep the foot relaxed. This is an effective way to stop a high-flying ball.

F. Shin Trapping: The shin trap is a method of stopping the ball with the shins. Stand just forward of the spot where the ball should strike the ground and allow it to strike the shins in flight or on the bounce. Use either one or both legs from the knee down, but do not allow the ball to strike the toe.

G. Body Trapping: The body trap is another method of gaining control of a ball in flight. Intercept the ball with any part of the upper body except the arms and hands. Keep the body relaxed and inclined toward the ball. To keep the ball from bouncing, move backward from it as it strikes the body. This will drop the ball at the feet in position for dribbling or passing.

H. Heading: Heading is the technique for changing the direction of the flight of a ball by butting it with the head. Tense the neck muscles and jump up to meet the ball. Butt the ball with the forehead at about the hairline to reverse its direction; use the side of the head to deflect it to the side. Always watch the ball, even during contact.

OFFENSIVE AND DEFENSIVE POSITIONS

The forwards usually play on the offensive half of the field and remain in a W formation. The fullbacks usually play on the defensive half of the field. The halfbacks are the backbone of the team; they move forward on the offense and back on defense. The goal keeper almost always remains within a few feet of the goal.

DRILLS TO DEVELOP BASIC SKILLS

Several skills are recommended to develop skill in kicking, passing, and shooting. The circle formation may be used for training in any of the basic skills. The ball may be headed or trapped as it is moved around or across the circle.

ABRIDGED RULES

A. A soccer team is composed of eleven players.

B. The player propels the ball by kicking it with the feet or any part of the legs, by butting it with his head, and by hitting it with any portion of his body except his arms or hands.

C. The goalkeeper is the only man allowed to use his hands on the ball, but he may only handle the ball in the goalkeeper's area. The term hands includes the whole arm from the point of the shoulder down.

D. A goal is made by causing the ball to cross completely the section of the goal line lying between the uprights and under the cross bar.

E. Each goal scores one point for the team scoring the goal.

F. The penalty for a foul committed anywhere on the playing field (except by the defensive team in its penalty area) is a free kick awarded to the team that committed the foul.

G. All opponents must be at least 10 yards from the ball when a free kick is taken.

H. The penalty for a foul committed by the defensive team in its penalty area is a penalty kick.

I. A penalty kick is a free kick at the goal from the spot 12 yards directly in front of the goal. The only players allowed within the penalty area at the time of the kick are the kicker and the defending goalkeeper.

J. An official game consists of four quarters.

K. Teams change goals at the end of every quarter.

L. In the event of a tie, an extra quarter is played.

M. After a ball has crossed a side line and has been declared out of play, it is put back into play by a free kick from the side line by a member of the team opposing the team that caused the ball to be out of bounds. The kick is taken from the point at which the ball crosses the side line as it goes out of bounds.

N. When the offensive team causes the ball to go behind the opposing team's goal line, excluding the portion between the goal posts, the opposing team is awarded a goal kick—a free kick taken within the goal area that must come out of the penalty area to be in play.

O. When the defensive team causes the ball to go behind its own goal line, excluding the portion between the goal posts, the opposing team is awarded a corner kick—a free kick taken by a member of the offensive team at the quarter circle at the corner flag-post nearest to where the ball went behind the goal line. The flat-post must not be removed.

P. The game is started and, after a goal has been scored, is resumed by placing the ball in the center of the mid-field line. Players must be on their side of the line until the ball is kicked. The ball must be kicked forward and must move a least two feet to be legal. The first kicker may not touch the ball twice in succession at the kick-off. The opposing team must be ten yards from the ball until it moves.

11

SOFTBALL

INTRODUCTION

  A. Softball is a game that is known in every corner of the country and has become a familiar sight in every sandlot in America. During and since World War II, it has become one of the principal physical training activities.

  B. Softball is patterned after baseball, but has different advantages because it requires less equipment and is easily adapted to every age group. It requires a smaller play area; the ball is larger and softer; and the bats are lighter, making them easier to handle. Because of its popularity, a majority of our young people have a general understanding of softball and softball rules, but only a comparative few possess the skill and knowledge to obtain the maximum benefit and satisfaction from the game

PLACE IN THE PROGRAM

  A. Softball is a sustaining type of activity. It does not require continuous exertion on the part of each player; however, it is an enjoyable and occasionally strenuous game that should be included in the physical training program.

  B. When a group already knows something about pitching, fielding, and batting, the instructor should give only a brief review of these fundamental skills, but place more emphasis on the rules and offensive and defensive strategy. Most of the time devoted to softball should be used for organized competition.

ORGANIZATION OF INSTRUCTION

When instruction is given on the basic skills and techniques, the students should first be shown the correct method of executing each skill. The class should then be divided into groups to practice. Ample time should be provided to familiarize each individual with the technique of playing each position as well as the basic skills necessary to play every position. When this instruction is completed, the class should be divided into teams for organized competition.

BASIC SKILLS

  A. Batting: Select a bat that balances easily—hands grasp the handle at a point where the butt is neither too heavy nor too light. For a right-handed batter, the left foot points at about a 45° angle toward the pitcher, and the right foot points toward homeplate. The feet are about 8 inches apart. The head and eyes face the pitcher, and the bat is over the right shoulder, hands away from the body. The batting position is slightly to the rear of the center of the plate. In swinging, keep the eyes on the ball, twisting at the waist. As a result of the twist, the arms will swing automatically. The power of the swing is developed with a snap of the wrists and the extension of the arms in the follow-through.

  B. Bunting: The stance for bunting is the same as for batting. When the ball leaves the pitcher's hand, immediately bring the bat from over the shoulder, moving the right hand slightly up the handle, until the bat is directly over the plate. Rotate the body so that it faces the pitcher. The feet are comfortably apart. Meet the ball squarely, absorbing the shock with the arms. Hold the edge of the bat perpendicular to the direction in which the ball is to be bunted.

C. Base Running: Upon hitting the ball, the runner must start quickly without watching where the ball goes. He should get to the first base as fast as possible and be ready to continue running at the coach's direction. Speed is the most important factor, but running the shortest distance between bases is also essential.

D. Sliding: Use the hook slide going into the base, with the body relaxed, extending either foot in a sweeping motion, touching the toe to the bag.

E. Catching: Assume the knee bend position, with the upper arms parallel to the ground, forearms vertical and palms down. As the ball strikes the mitt, grasp it with the bare hand. On high pitches, cup the fingers of the bare hand to prevent injury. On low pitches, extend the palms toward the pitcher with the thumbs down. Always avoid pointing the fingers toward the pitcher. The catcher must not sacrifice accuracy for speed in throwing to bases and must learn through experience when he can throw a player out at base.

F. Pitching: Pitching, to a large degree, determines a team's defensive strength, and pitching can only be developed through practice. To hold the ball, grasp it loosely with the fingers, the index, middle, and third finger on one side and the thumb and fourth finger on the other side. The most effective manner of pitching is the windmill pitch. To start the wind-up, face the homeplate with both feet on the rubber. The ball is held in front with both hands. Raise the left foot to the rear as the right arm swings backward. The body pivots to the right, the left hand is extended and balances the motion, and the head and eyes remain on the catcher's glove. When the right arm reaches the nine o'clock position, step forward with the left foot directly toward homeplate, swing the arm forward, and twist the body to the left. With a snap of the wrist on the underhand swing, release the ball and follow through. Control is very important and must be gained through practice.

G. Infield Playing: An infielder must anticipate at all times what he should do in case he has to play the ball. On batted ground balls, he should play the ball to his front. Field each ground ball with the feet apart, hands well out in front. When the ball strikes the glove, secure it with the bare hand. The hands and arms should relax, and the arms should be drawn backward toward the right hip preparatory to the throw.

H. Outfield Playing: An outfielder should be alert and fast and able to judge the ball so he can get in the best position to catch it. It takes practice to become a successful fielder. To catch a fly ball, he extends the arms forward, forming a cup with the hands. He keeps his eyes on the ball until he has firm possession of it. He catches ground balls in the same way as the infielder (see G above).

DRILLS

A. Pitching and Catching: Divide the class into two lines fifty feet apart; one side will pitch, the other will catch. Make corrections on form for both pitching and catching. emphasize form and control. Change over.

B. Infield Play: Divide the class into seven-man groups. Place each group in a separate area, simulating (if necessary) the softball diamond. Designate a first, second, and third baseman, and a shortstop. Choose one man to hit balls and one to catch at homeplate. The player who hits balls first calls a play such as first base, double play, throw it home, etc. He then hits a ground ball to one of the infielders who, in turn, carries out the prescribed play. Demand enthusiasm and hustle. Change over occasionally and allow each man to play each position.

C. Outfield Play: Place seven men in the outfield, but do not designate definite positions. Have a player hit both fly and ground balls to the field. Use one player to catch balls at homeplate. After each ball has been played, have it relayed back to the hitter. Change positions so that each player has an opportunity to play in the outfield.

D. Base Running: Divide the class into fifteen-man groups. Time each runner in a complete circuit of bases. Stimulate competition. Critique each runner.

E. Hitting and Bunting: Divide the class into regular nine-man teams. Place one team in the infield to shag balls. The players on the other team take turns at bat, hitting ten balls each. On the last pitch, they lay down a bunt and run to first base, trying to beat the throw. Change over.

OFFENSIVE AND DEFENSIVE STRATEGY

A. Offensive: Hit only good balls (balls in the strike zone). Runners should run out fly balls at top speed, in case the ball is dropped or an error is committed. There is a better possibility of stealing a base than of the next batter hitting safely. Do not hesitate in stealing. Do not attempt to steal third base when two men are out, because a runner should be able to score from second base on a hit or on an error. It is best to attempt to steal second base with two outs. With no outs and runners on first and second base, a bunt combined with a double steal is good strategy. A runner can usually score from third base on a fly ball or on an error.

B. Defensive: A play should always back up another player receiving a throw at a base, or a player attempting to make a play on a fly or ground ball. The player who is nearest the ball should call for it and make the catch or play. Each player should be aware of the situation and know exactly what to do if he receives the ball. Receive bunts, flys, and ground balls with both hands. Have firm possession of the ball before attempting a throw. On force plays, do not stand on the base. It is better to make certain of one out, rather than risk an error in trying for a double play. When a shorter throw can put a runner out at base, it is best to attempt the shorter throw. With runners on first and second base, it is better to force out at third than to try a double play from second to first base. An outfielder should throw the ball directly to the spot where the play is likely to be made, unless it is a long fly and a relay appears to be quicker.

SPEEDBALL

INTRODUCTION AND GENERAL DESCRIPTION

Speedball is a game that offers vigorous and varied action with plenty of scoring opportunities. It is easy to learn and provides spontaneous fun. Little equipment is needed—a ball is all that is absolutely necessary. Speedball combines the kicking, trapping, and intercepting elements of soccer; the passing game of basketball; and the punting, drop-kicking, and scoring pass of football. Two teams of eleven men each play the game under official rules, but any number of players may successfully constitute a team. An inflated leather ball, usually a soccer ball, is used. The playing field is a football field with a football goal post at each end. The game starts with a soccer-type kickoff. The kicking team tries to retain possession of the ball and advance it toward the opposite goal by passing or kicking it. Running with the ball is not allowed, so there is no tackling or interference. When the ball touches the ground, it cannot be picked up with the hands or caught on the bounce, but must be played as in soccer until it is raised into the air directly from a kick; then the hands are again eligible for use. When the ball goes out of bounds over the side lines, it is given to a player of the team opposite that forcing the ball out, and is put into play with a basketball throw-in; when it goes over the end line without a score, it is given to a player of the opposing team who may either pass or kick it onto the field. When two opposing players are contesting the possession of a held ball, the official tosses the ball up between them as in basketball. Points are scored by kicking the ball under the crossbar of the goal posts, drop-kicking the ball over the crossbar, completing a forward pass into the end zone for a touchdown, or by kicking the ball under the crossbar of the goal posts on a penalty kick.

PLACE IN THE PROGRAM

Speedball, like soccer, should be introduced into the physical training program during the latter part of the toughening stage and used as a competitive activity in the sustaining stage. It may be played any time the weather permits, but it is primarily a spring or fall activity.

BASIC SKILLS

   A. Soccer Techniques
      1. Kicking
      2. Passing
      3. Heading
      4. Trapping

   B. Football Techniques
      1. Punting
      2. Drop-kicking
      3. Forward passing

   C. Basketball Techniques
      1. Passing
      2. Receiving
      3. Pivoting

   D. Kickups and Lifts: The kickup is a play in which the player lifts the ball into the air with his feet so that he may legally play the ball with his hands. The kickup is generally used to make the transition from ground play to aerial play. The technique of making the play depends upon whether the ball is rolling or stationary. To kick up a ball rolling or bouncing toward the player, the foot is held on the ground with the toe drawn down until the ball rolls onto the foot, then the foot is raised, projecting the ball upward. If the ball is stationary, the player rolls it backward with one foot, then places the foot where the ball will roll onto it. He can then lift the ball with that foot. If a ball is running away from the player, he should stop it with a foot and play it as a stationary ball. There is also a method of raising the ball by standing over it with a foot on either side. He presses his feet against the ball and jumps into the air, propelling the ball into his hands.

OFFENSIVE POSITIONS AND STRATEGY

The positions of the players in speedball are much the same as in soccer. However, some of the positions are designated by different names. There are eleven players on each team. The forward line is composed of five players: the right end, right forward, center, left forward, and left end. The second line consists of right halfback, fullback, and left halfback. In the next line is the right guard and left guard. The player who defends the goal is the goal guard. The strategy employed in speedball during offensive play is very similar to that of soccer.

DEFENSIVE PLAY

There are two types of defensive formations in speedball: man-for-man and position defense. Man-for-man defense is recommended for beginning players.

ABRIDGED RULES

A. The Field: 360 feet long and 160 feet wide (a regulation football field).

B. Players: Eleven on a team. The goal guard has no special privileges.

C. Time: Ten-minute quarters, two minutes between. Ten minutes between halves. Five minutes for extra overtime periods. (Begin first overtime by a jump ball (see G.3. below) at center, same goals; change goals in the event of a second overtime period.)

D. Winner of Toss: The winner of the toss has the choice of kicking, receiving, or defending a specific goal.

E. Starting Second and Fourth Quarters: The ball is given to the team that had possession at the end of the previous quarter, out of bounds, as in basketball.

F. Half: The team that received at the start of the first half kicks off at the beginning of the second half.

G. The Game: The game is started with a kickoff from the middle line (50-yard line), both teams being required to remain back of their respective restraining lines until the ball is kicked. The ball must travel forward.

1. The most characteristic feature of the playing rules of speedball is the differentiation between a fly ball (or aerial ball) and a ground ball. A player is not permitted to touch a ground ball with his hands and must play it as in soccer. A fly ball is one that has risen into the air directly from the foot of a player (example: punt, drop-kick, place-kick, or kickup). Such a ball may be caught with the hands

provided the catch is made before the ball strikes the ground again. A kickup is a ball that is so kicked by a player that he can catch it himself. A bounce from the ground may not be touched with the hand because it has touched the ground since being kicked. This rule prohibits thee ordinary basketball dribble, but one overhead dribble (throwing the ball into the air and advancing to catch it before it hits the ground) is permitted.

2. If a team causes the ball to go out of bounds over the side lines, a free thrown-in (any style) is given to the opposing team. When the ball goes over the end line without scoring, it is given to the opponents who may pass or kick from out of bounds at that point.

3. In case two players are contesting the possession of a held ball, even in the end zone, a tie ball is declared and the ball is tossed up between them.

4. The kick-off is made from any place on or behind the 50-yard line. Team A (the kicking team) must be behind the ball when it is kicked. Team B must stay back of its restraining line (ten yards' distance) until the ball is kicked (penalty—a violation). The ball must go forward before A may play it (penalty—violation). Kick off out of bounds to opponents at that spot. A kick-off touched by B and going out of bounds, no impetus added, still belongs to B. A kick-off, in possession and control of B and then fumbled out of bounds, belongs to A at that spot. A field goal from kick-off (under crossbar, etc.) scores 3 points.

H. Scoring Methods

1. Field Goal (3 points): A soccer-type kick, in which a ground ball is kicked under the crossbar and between the goal posts from the field of play or end zone. (A punt going straight through is not a field goal for it is not a ground ball. The ball must hit the ground first.). A drop-kick from the field of play that goes under a crossbar does not count as a field goal. A drop-kick from the end zone that goes under the crossbar counts as a field goal; if it goes over the crossbar, it is ruled as a touch back.

2. Drop-kick (2 points): A scoring drop-kick must be made from the field of play and go over the crossbar and between the uprights. The ball must hit the ground before it is kicked (usually with the instep).

3. End Goal (1 point): This is a ground ball which receives its impetus (kicked or legally propelled by the body) from any player, offensive or defensive, in the end zone and passes over the end line but not between the goal posts.

4. Penalty Kick (1 point): This is a ball kicked from the penalty mark that goes between the goal posts and under the crossbar. The penalty mark is placed directly in front of the goal at the center of the goal line.

5. Touchdown (1 point): A touchdown is a forward pass from the field of play completed in the end zone. The player must be entirely in the end zone. If he is on the goal line or has one foot in the field of play and the other in the end zone, the ball is declared out of bounds. If a forward pass is missed, the ball continues in

play but must be returned to the field of play before another forward pass or drop-kick may be made.

I. Substitutions: Substitutions may be made any time when the ball is not in play. If a player is withdrawn, he may not return during that same period.

J. Time Out: Three legal time-outs of two minutes each are permitted each team during the game.

K. Fouls

   1. Personal (four disqualify): Kicking, tripping, charging, pushing, holding, blocking, or unnecessary roughness of any kind, such as running into an opponent from behind. Kicking at a fly ball and thereby kicking an opponent.

   2. Technical: Illegal substitution, more than three time-outs in a game, unsportsmanlike conduct, unnecessarily delaying the game.

   3. Violation: Traveling with the ball, touching a ground ball with the hands or arms, double overhead dribble, violating tie ball, and kicking or kneeing a fly ball before catching it.

   4. Penalties: (The offended player shall attempt the kick.)

	Penalty	Location
Personal	In field of play	1 kick with no follow-up
Technical	In field of play	1 kick with no follow-up
Violation	In field of play	Out of bounds to opponent
Personal	In end zone	2 kick with no follow-up on last kick
Technical	In end zone	1 kick with no follow-up
Violation	In end zone	1 kick with no follow-up

l. Summary of Fouls

   1. Fouls in the field of play allow no follow-up while fouls in the end zone always allow follow-up.

   2. On penalty kicks, with no follow-up, only the kicker and goalie are involved.

   3. On penalty kicks, with a follow-up, the kicking side is behind the ball and the defending side behind the end line or in the field of play. No one is allowed in the end zone or between the goal post except the goal guard. The kicker cannot play the ball again until after another player plays it, and he must make an actual attempt at goal.

TOUCH FOOTBALL

INTRODUCTION

Touch football has become a major active game on the lower levels of competition. Considering its similarity to football and yet its comparative simplicity, it is easy to understand the popularity of the game. The modification of regulation football rules for touch football eliminates the necessity for much special equipment, training, and professional leadership. Touch football encourages participation, reduces the number of injuries, and simplifies the teaching of fundamental rules, techniques, and skills.

PLACE IN THE PROGRAM

Touch football is an excellent conditioning activity, and it should be included in both the physical training and intramural programs. It may be used in the latter part of the toughening stage and during the sustaining stage of physical conditioning. It should be played in the fall when the interest in football is at its peak. Any level field can be used. Goal posts are desirable but not absolutely necessary.

ORGANIZATION OF INSTRUCTION

Most men know something about football, but not all have had an opportunity to play. Several short periods should be devoted to the instruction of all men in the basic fundamentals. A desirable method is to give five to ten minutes of instruction at the beginning of each football period and follow it by actual play.

BASIC SKILLS

A. Offensive Stance: Touch football emphasizes speed; therefore, a high offensive stance should be used to facilitate a fast getaway. The feet should be about shoulder width apart and parallel, knees bent, thighs just above the horizontal and back nearly parallel with the ground. The head and eyes are up, and the right hand is extended straight downward, the fingers curled under, the thumb toward the rear. The left arm rests on the left thigh. There are many variations of this basic stance that may be used. The general principles are: Keep the feet spread for balance, the body under control, and the head up with the eyes on an opponent or the ball.

B. Defensive Stance: This type stance may be similar to the offensive stance or somewhat higher to allow for better visibility and free use of the hands to ward off blockers. The same principles of balance, body control, and vision used in the offensive stance are applicable to the defensive stance.

C. Blocking: Touch football rules do not permit the blocker to have both feet off the ground at the same time (flying block); therefore, the blocker should maintain a wide base for shoulder, upright, or cross-body blocks. For the shoulder block, the hands should be close to the chest, the elbows raised sideward, the feet under the body and widely spread, the head up, and the buttocks low. Upon contact, the feet should be moved rapidly in short, choppy steps to force the body forward, thus keeping the shoulder in contact with the opponent. The upright block is useful in the open field and is executed by the player while standing nearly erect. The feet are widely spread, knees slightly bent, the trunk inclined slightly forward, and the head erect. The arms are raised, and the hands are placed on the chest, forearms forward to contact the opponent. Due to the nature of the block, the opponent is contacted above the waist.

In performing the cross-body block, the blocker uses the hip to contact the opponent, usually in the area of the thighs. The execution of this type of block requires the blocker to throw his head, shoulders, and arms past the target area, thus bringing his hip into contact with his opponent. Then, assisted by movement of the hands and feet which are in contact with the ground, he forces the opponent backward or down. The shoulder, upright, or cross-body blocks may be used in the line or in the open field.

D. Ball Carrying: The first point to stress in ball carrying is the grip of the ball. The ball is placed in the arm with its long axis parallel to the forearm. It is held firmly and close to the body. The hand grips the lower point of the ball with the fingers spread to form a firm grip. It is difficult to teach the fine points of ball carrying in a few hours of instruction. Stress the principles. Teach runners to carry the ball in the arm away from the opponent. The runner should be cautioned to follow his interference and to keep his head up so he can avoid his opponents.

E. Forward Passing: Forward passing is one of the principal means of advancing the ball in touch football. Teach the method of gripping or holding the ball with the fingers spread on the laces and toward the end of the ball, cocking the arm with the hand holding the ball close to the head and the wrist rotated so that the rear point of the ball is pointing toward the head. The ball is delivered with a baseball catcher's peg motion, by extending the arm and imparting a spiral to the ball. To make a successful forward pass, it is usually best for the passer to have the feet spread comfortably and in contact with the ground, the free hand extended to aid the balance. He throws the ball to a spot where the receiver can catch it without breaking his stride. Do not allow beginners to attempt jump passes, as the successful throwing of this type of pass requires the skill of an experienced forward passer.

F. Pass Receiving: To catch a forward pass requires the receiver to keep his eyes on the ball, to run to the spot where he can reach the ball, to catch it without breaking stride, and to take it out of the air by relaxing the hands as the ball strikes. In receiving a pass over the shoulder, the little fingers are facing, with the thumbs outward and all fingers spread. In catching a pass while facing the passer, the receiver should catch a high pass with the thumbs facing and the little fingers out; and a low pass with the little fingers facing and the thumbs pointing outward.

DRILLS TO DEVELOP FUNDAMENTALS

It is recommended that the time available for instruction in the fundamentals be used in teaching the following skills: stance, shoulder block, cross-body block, forward passing, and pass receiving.

A. Stance Drill: Use the extended rectangular formation. Demonstrate the stance and tell the men they will execute the drill by the numbers. At the count of one, place the feet in position. At the count of two, bend the knees and trunk. At the count of three, lean forward and place one hand on the ground. After checking for errors and making corrections, command "UP" and execute the drill again. Have the men do this several times before progressing to the next drill.

B. Blocking Drills: All the blocks may be practiced by forming the class into two lines facing one another and having the men pair off. Explain the drill, demonstrate the block desired, and designate one line as blockers and the other as opponents. After several practice blocks, have the blockers become the opponents and the opponents become the blockers. During the course of the drill, emphasize the three phases of blocking: the approach, contact, and follow-through.

C. Forward Passing Drill: Form the class in groups of ten men each. The groups form two lines with the men about ten feet apart and the two lines ten to fifteen yards apart. Using at least one ball to a group, practice grip, balance, throwing with a spiral, and follow-through. The ball is thrown by each man, in turn, to the next man in the opposite line who catches it and throws.

D. Passing and Receiving Drill: Each of the groups is formed as for the drill outlined in C above. One man, the center, is stationed between the two files with the ball. One file is designated as passers and the other as receivers. The center snaps the ball to the first passer. He passes to the first receiver who runs down the field at the snap of the ball. The receiver catches the pass and returns the ball to the center. Upon his return, the receiver joins the "passer" file and the passer joins the "receiver" file. This rotation continues until all men have an opportunity to throw and receive forward passes.

E. Other Drills: If time permits, other fundamental drills may be included, such as snapping the ball from center, kicking, lateral passing, and other individual skills of a specialty nature.

OFFENSIVE FORMATIONS AND PLAY

A. A nine-man team is recommended. Three offensive formations are suggested for this size team. Of the three formations suggested, the double wing-back is the best.

B. To complete the instruction in offensive play, it will be necessary to insure that some member of the team can perform the individual specialties. These special skills are passing the ball from center, punting, free kicking for kick-offs, backfield pivots, handoffs, etc.

C. Men like to develop their own plays and should be encouraged to do so. Time must be made available for them to practice such plays before using them in a game.

DEFENSIVE PLAY

The class should be shown several defensive formations. Four different ones are applicable for the nine-man team. The selection of a defense depends upon the opponent's offense. The 4-2-2-1 and the 5-1-2-1 are better pass defense formations than the 4-3-2 and the 5-2-2. The latter formations are weak "down the middle." However, the 4-3-2 and 5-2-2 are stronger against a running attack. If fewer men are employed on a team, the defense could be altered by eliminating either linemen or backs, as required.

ORGANIZATION AND ADMINISTRATION

A. The instructor may divide the class into teams from the roster or by selecting team captains who, in turn, choose the remaining members of their teams.

B. The officials may be assistant instructors or selected individuals from the class. It is suggested that there should be at least one official for each game that is played.

Close supervision of play and strict enforcement of rules are necessary to prevent injuries from excessive roughness.

C. To insure the success of touch football in a physical training period, the teams should be organized into a class league to stimulate interest and competition, and to select the championship team.

D. There should be one ball for each fifteen men.

E. The area for practice and play should be grassed and level. The field should conform as nearly as possible to the size specified in paragraph 9.A.1.

RULES

It is important that the participants know the rules that govern touch football. It increases the players' enjoyment in the activity, lessens the chance of injury, and results in an organized contest. Official National Collegiate Athletic Association football rules shall govern all play except those special rules pertinent to touch football, as stated in the following subparagraphs.

A. Rule I: Field and Equipment
  1. Section 1 – Field: The game shall be played on a regulation football field with goal posts. When space is limited, the dimensions of the field may be reduced to 300 feet long by 120 feet wide.
  2. Section 2 – Uniforms: Distinctive jerseys, shorts, sweat suits, or trousers, and basketball shoes or regulation footwear may be worn. Pads, helmets, and cleated shoes are not authorized.

B. Rule II: Length of Game
  1. Section 1 – Periods: The game shall be played in four periods each ten minutes in length, with a one-minute interval between the first and second and the third and fourth periods; and with a ten-minute interval between the second and third periods.

  2. Section 2 – Contest: By mutual agreement of opposing coaches or captains, before the start of contest, the length of the periods may be shortened or lengthened.

  3. Section 3 – Time Out: Time out shall be taken
      a. After a touchdown, field goal, safety, or touch back.
      b. During a try for a point.
      c. After an incomplete forward pass.
      d. When the ball goes out of bounds.
      e. During the enforcement or declination of penalties.

C. Rule III: Players and Substitutes

  1. Section 1 – Players (nine-man team): Each team shall consist of nine players. The offensive team shall have a minimum of five players on the scrimmage line when the ball is snapped. Note: The following diagram designates the position of the players:

22

    END   GUARD   CENTER   GUARD   END
                        QUARTERBACK
          HALFBACK   HALFBACK
                        FULLBACK

2. Section 2 – Players (six-man game): Each team shall consist of six players. The offensive team shall have a minimum of three players on the scrimmage line when the ball is snapped. Note: The following diagram designates the position of the players.

    END   CENTER   END
  HALFBACK   HALFBACK
      FULLBACK

3. Section 3 – Substitutions: Unrestricted substitutions may be made when
   a. The ball is dead.
   b. The clock is running, provided substitutions are completed and the ball is snapped within 25 seconds after the ball is ready for play.

D. Rule IV: Playing Regulations

1. Section 1: Starting the game and putting ball in play after any score shall be as prescribed by the NCAA Football Rule Book, with exception of Rule 4, Sections 2 and 3.
2. Section 2 – Kick-off: The receiving team, in a nine-man game, shall have three players within five yards of its own restraining line until the ball is kicked.
3. Section 3 – Restriction: In a six-man game, the only restriction on the receiving team is that all players must remain back of their own restraining line until the ball is kicked.
4. Section 4 – Fumbled Ball: A ball that is fumbled and touches the ground during a run, kick, or lateral pass play, may not be advanced by either team. The ball may be touched and recovered by any player. It shall be dead and in possession of the player who first touches it after it strikes the ground.
   Note: Players shall be warned against diving on fumbled balls and may be penalized for unnecessary roughness.
5. Section 5 – Fumbled Ball or Lateral Pass: A fumbled ball or lateral pass, intercepted or recovered before it touches the ground, may be advanced by any player.
6. Section 6 – Downed Ball By Legal Touch: The player in possession of the ball is downed and the ball is dead when such player is touched by an opponent with both hands simultaneously above the waist and below the head.
7. Section 7 – Forward Passing: One forward pass may be made during each scrimmage play from behind the passer's scrimmage line.
8. Section 8 – Eligible Receivers: All players of offensive and defensive teams are eligible to receive forward passes. Two or more receives may successively touch a forward pass.

E. Rule V – Fouls and Penalties. Section 1 – Use of hands and arms. For both offense and defense, as prescribed in NCAA Football Rule Book.

VOLLEYBALL

INTRODUCTION

    A. Volleyball is a popular sport. The game entails much physical activity, yet it is not strenuous. It is, therefore, a game for young and older men alike, for beginners and for skilled players. It may be played indoors or outdoors on any type of terrain. As an informal activity, volleyball can be played by any number of men; as an organized activity, it provides, as few other sports do, a game for twelve men to play in a limited area.

    B. While volleyball requires no great skill to play, it does permit a high degree of proficiency. A man naturally gets more enjoyment when he knows the game and plays it well. For this reason, instruction in the basic skills should be provided.

ORGANIZATION

Usually a ten- to fifteen-minute period of instruction, followed by scrimmage during the first three or four classes is enough to teach the basic skills, rules, and techniques of volleyball. More time can be given to teaching basic skills, if available, but the emphasis is on competitive play rather than on formal instruction. It is best to lecture and demonstrate to the entire class, then divide the class into smaller groups for practice. For drills and scrimmages, divide the class so that there will be from twelve to twenty-four men to each court. One court may be used for instruction by allowing twelve players at a time to execute the drill while the other class members observe, act as coaches, or retrieve balls. After the instruction phase of training has been completed, divide the class into six-man teams. Organize the teams on the basis of ability. All teams should be as nearly equal as possible.

PLACE IN THE PROGRAM

Volleyball may be used occasionally as a competitive activity during the sustaining stage. It is a year-round sport, but it should be included in the physical training program only when it is impractical to conduct a more strenuous activity. It is an excellent self-interest activity.

    A. Passing

        1. Handling the Low Ball: A ball that is lower than the waist is one of the easiest to hit, but is also a frequent cause of the fouls of holding or carrying the ball. The best position for handling a low ball is to have the feet staggered, knees flexed, and arms flexed at the elbows and rotated so the thumbs are pointing outward, the palms up. When the fingers contact the ball, the entire body reacts in a lifting motion. The arms and hands swing upward in a scooping action. It is important that the fingers, not the palms, contact the ball, and that the ball is batted not thrown.

        2. Handling the High Ball: The chest pass is the most effective method of playing the ball. To receive the ball, the feet are staggered, knees are flexed, and the body is tilted forward. The elbows are raised sideward to a point in line with the shoulders. The wrists are extended in line with the forearm and the arms, wrists, and hands are rotated inward. To pass the ball, the hands are chest high, thumbs pointing inward. The fingers are flexed, forming a cup, allowing them to contact the ball. On contact with the ball, the wrists are snapped while the fingers and elbows are

pushed upward, sending the ball upward. A high ball is much easier to handle than a low one.

B. Serving
   1. The Underhand Serve: Take a position behind the back line facing the net, left foot forward, holding the ball in the palm of the left hand. The left knee is flexed, the right knee is straight. Swing the right arm back and at the same time move the left hand (holding the ball) across the body in line with the right hip. Then swing the right arm forward hitting the ball off of the left hand with the palm of the right hand, raising the hips and arching the back in the same motion. Be certain to swing the right arm in a straight line, or the ball will be difficult to control.

   2. Placement of the Serve: When the opposition is in formation, the server should try to place the ball in the right or left back area, and not near the net.

C. Setting It Up: A setup is a ball into the air near the net by one player, so a teammate may hit or "spike" it sharply downward into the opponent's court. The chest pass is the best pass to use. The ball is sent approximately ten feet into the air toward the spiker so it will descend from four to twenty inches from the net.

D. Spiking: The spike is a leap into the air and a sharp downward hitting of the ball into the opponent's court. A spiker must be able to spring easily from the floor, judge the movement of the ball, and strike it with a downward movement of his arm. To jump from the floor, step off with one foot and jump with the other. Stand with the right or left side to the net, facing the setup man. Much depends upon the setup man to place the ball in the proper position. The spiker jumps into the air and strikes the ball above its center so as to drive it downward. A snapping movement of the arm and wrist will drive the ball forward and downward with power and control. Aim for a weak spot in the opponent's defense.

E. Blocking: The block is a technique of defense used to prevent a spiker from driving the ball across the net. It is an attempt by one or more defensive players at the net to block a hard hit shot by using the force of the ball to send it immediately back into the opponent's court. An effective block is for forwards on the defensive team to spring into the air at the time of the spike, placing both hands and arms in the expected path of the ball. An effective block tends to upset the offense and presents another element for the spiker to worry about. To be effective, the blocker must anticipate the path of the ball and time his block with the spike.

DRILLS TO DEVELOP BASIC SKILLS

A. Passing
   1. Divide the class into twenty-four-man groups. Have them form a circle and begin passing a ball around the circle trying to prevent it from touching the floor.

   2. Divide each group with twelve men on a side facing the net. Form four ranks per side, with the first ranks passing the ball back and forth over the net until a pass is incomplete. Then have the second rank move up. Place the groups in a regular playing formation concentrating only on passing, using both the chest pass and the low pass.

B. Serving: Break the men into two groups—one line to act as servers, the other as retrievers. Change over frequently giving each man a chance. When the men can control the serve, have each server try to place the ball in the various areas of the court.

C. Spiking: Have two lines on one side of the court facing the net. One line is the spiking line, the other is the setup line. One man from each line moves up to the net at one time. The spiker tosses to the setup, the setup sets the ball up for spiker, and the spiker drives it over the net. Rotate the lines.

OFFENSIVE PLAY

A. Each member of a good offensive team should
   1. Be able to serve.
   2. Know the capabilities and weaknesses of each of his teammates.
   3. Have an understanding of all offensive plays.
   4. Be able to analyze the opponent's weaknesses.
   5. Always know what area of the court he is responsible for.
   6. Be ready to "back up" a teammate receiving the ball.

B. The big offensive power is the spiker. It is also necessary, however, to build a well-balanced team that can serve, pass, and "set up."

DEFENSIVE PLAY

The reception and handling of serves and spikes is the primary duty of the team on defense.

A. Receiving the Serve: The forwards move to the rear of their area. The left and right backs cover the rear, the center back plays slightly forward of the other two backs.

B. Blocking: The block is made by the center forward and either the right or left forward. The forward not executing the block must cover the position left vacant.

ABRIDGED RULES

A. The volleyball court is 30 feet wide by 60 feet long

B. The top of the net is 8 feet high.

C. A volleyball team consists of six players.

D. A match consists of the best two out of three games.

E. The first team scoring 15 points wins the game, provided that they have two points more than their opponents.

F. A deuce game is a game in which both teams score 14 points. The game is continued until one team obtains a 2-point advantage over the other

G. Only the serving team can score. If the serving team commits a fault, it loses the serve to the opposing team.

H. The team receiving the ball for service rotates one position in a clockwise direction.

I. The ball is put into play by serving from behind the back line.

J. A served ball touching the net results in the loss of the serve. At any other time during play, a ball touching the net is still in play.

K. The ball is out of play when it touches the ground or goes outside one of the boundary lines.

L. All line balls are good.

M. The players must hit or bat the ball; they may not throw, lift, or scoop it.

N. A player may not touch the ball with any part of the body below the knees.

O. A player may not play (touch) the ball twice in succession. In receiving a hard-driven spike, a defensive player may make several contacts with the ball even if they are not simultaneous. All such contacts, however, must constitute one continuous play, and all must be above the knees.

P. The ball may be touched no more than three times on one side of the net before being returned across the net to the opposing team.

Q. A player must not touch or reach across the net.

R. A player must not cross the line under the net; he may touch it, however.

S. For complete official volleyball rules, see the United States Volleyball Association: <u>Volleyball Official Guide</u>.